THE **PROPAGATION HANDBOOK**

HILTON CARTER

THE PROPAGATION HANDBOOK

A GUIDE TO PROPAGATING HOUSEPLANTS

CICO BOOKS
LONDON NEW YORK

Photographer Hilton Carter
Senior designer Megan Smith
Senior commissioning editor Annabel Morgan
Editor Sophie Devlin
Art director Sally Powell
Creative director Leslie Harrington
Head of production Patricia Harrington

Published in 2024 by CICO Books
An imprint of Ryland Peters & Small Ltd
20–21 Jockey's Fields
London WC1R 4BW
and 341 E 116th St
New York, NY 10029
www.rylandpeters.com

10 9 8 7 6 5 4 3 2 1

Text © Hilton Carter 2024
Design and photography
© CICO Books 2024

A CIP catalog record for
this book is available from
the Library of Congress
and the British Library.

ISBN: 978-1-80065-310-8

Printed in China

WINDOW DIRECTION AND LIGHT LEVELS

Understanding the types of light you have
in your home will make a big difference
to the choice of plants you can place in
those areas. Here's a breakdown of the
types of light your plants will receive in
the northern hemisphere, depending on
the direction in which a window is facing
(these directions will be reversed if you
live in the southern hemisphere):

NORTHERN EXPOSURE
Medium to bright indirect
light

NORTHEAST EXPOSURE
Medium to bright indirect
light. Depending on the
time of year, direct
sunlight in the morning

NORTHWEST EXPOSURE
Bright indirect light

EASTERN EXPOSURE
Direct morning sunlight
to bright indirect light

SOUTHERN EXPOSURE
Bright indirect light
to medium light

SOUTHEAST EXPOSURE
Bright indirect light

SOUTHWEST EXPOSURE
Bright indirect light to
direct afternoon sunlight

WESTERN EXPOSURE
Bright indirect light to
direct afternoon sunlight

CONTENTS

INTRODUCTION

They say that when you give a piece of yourself to someone, you're sharing the world. OK, I've never heard anyone say that verbatim, but I believe those words to be true. Because when you're able to gift something that celebrates who you are and the things you care for, that ultimately tells the story of you: you're gifting YOUR world. In The Propagation Handbook, I'm so excited to gift you my world.

Perhaps what I love most about the practice of propagating is that you're able to share a passion for plants with the ones you love. It's a common experience that many of us find our way into plant parenting through propagation. A family member takes a cutting from a favorite plant and gifts it to someone else in the family, who then takes a cutting from that plant, and in that way it is handed down from one generation to the next. That first plant, known as the "mother plant," finds its way from home to home, and more importantly, from heart to heart.

For me, propagating houseplants is one of the most fun and rewarding ways to add plants to my collection and life to my home. There are different techniques for propagating different species, but when you are equipped with the right tools and knowledge, the process can be quite simple.

I call propagating the gift that keeps on giving. When you take a cutting, it will grow and can eventually be propagated itself. And when you share a cutting with someone and they gather the knowledge of what type of vessel it should be placed in and how to care for it, they see the magic happen when they finally place it in water and watch as the roots grow and develop. That new plant parent goes through the process of potting the young plant in soil, nurturing it, and watching it mature. A bond is slowly created and eventually becomes so strong that the individual is transformed into a plant lover and filled with the desire to share that joy with others.

I know this from personal experience. It was propagating a small stem of a golden pothos (*Epipremnum aureum*) that first opened my heart and mind to the beauty of plant parenting and lit the

spark within that led me to share my passion for plants with so many others. I can still remember the feeling I had when I first saw roots developing from that pothos—it was a "wow" moment. I truly believe that I wouldn't be where I am today, not just as a plant stylist and plant parent, but even as a husband, father, son, or friend, if it wasn't for the process of learning to care for plants.

You see, for me, discovering how to propagate a plant from a cutting changed my life. That may sound hyperbolic, but it's something I know to be true. The process of propagation slowly revealed to

STATE OF MIND
In the greenhouse, I am always focused on tending to my plants (above). Here, I'm looking for nodes on a *Philodendron squamiferum* and observing where to make a cut. When I take the time to be mindful, caring for my plants feels more like a meditation than a chore.

me that I was doing more than just nurturing plants—I was also nurturing myself. I wasn't just cutting plants for the sake of pruning and propagating. It went much deeper than that. At the same time, I was pruning back my ego and propagating humility and happiness. And it was that realization that made me want to write this book.

There are different techniques for successfully propagating different types of plants. Each of these methods requires an understanding of the plant you're working with to give the new cutting the best chance of survival. In this book I'll answer your questions, such as "Where is the best place on a plant to make a cut?", "Do you place the cutting in regular water right away", "How long will it take before my cutting grows roots?", and all the other queries that tend to arise during the propagation process. These are just some of the questions I had when I first got started on this journey, and I will share all the answers with you in this book.

I have found tremendous happiness in propagating and sharing all kinds of plants with my friends and family over the years. In *The Propagation Handbook*, I hope to equip you with the necessary knowledge and tools to propagate happiness for yourself and those around you.

TOOLS OF THE TRADE

When it comes to achieving the best results in the propagating process, in order to set yourself up for success it's important to have the right equipment. I can promise you that you won't have much success trying to take a cutting from your plant with a spoon. However, the good news is that it really doesn't require many tools to propagate new plant babies.

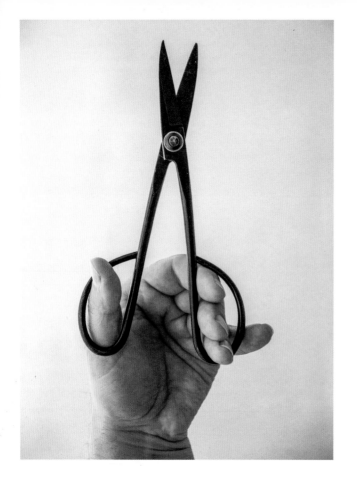

PPE (PROTECTIVE PLANT EQUIPMENT)
Here is my wall of wonders (opposite). I like to keep tools accessible and in sight for on-the-spot treatment of my plants. The tools include a brush, sanitized shears (also see left), plant tape, and, of course, a trowel. Having a place for these tools makes plant care much simpler.

The essential tools are a sharp blade to make the cut, the right vessel in which to place the cutting while its roots are developing, a watering can, and the right planter to pot the cutting into once its root system has developed. Whether or not you're already a plant parent, like many of us are nowadays, these tools are readily and inexpensively available, making it easy for anyone to get started.

SHEARS

It all starts with the initial cut of the plant, and using the right tool here can be key to propagation success. You can use craft scissors, a knife, or traditional pruning shears/secateurs. What's important is that the blades of your tool are clean and sharp—the sharper, the better. A sharp blade creates a swift, clean cut that allows for greater success when the plant produces roots. A dull blade and blunt cut can

rip and mangle the tissues of the plant, making it more difficult for the cut end to push out roots and for the mother plant to push out new growth.

Deciding what type of shears to use to make the cut will depend on the size of the plant you are taking cuttings from. Scissors and pruning shears are fine for snipping the slender stems of vine plants or taking leaf cuttings from small plants, but a sharp knife or pair of loppers may be required when taking a cutting from a tree-like plant or large cactus.

Once you've made the cut, it's important to clean the blades afterward, for two reasons. Firstly, when you make the cut, the plant may release sap that could be toxic to kids and pets. So wipe any sap away that could potentially harm a curious cat or puzzled pup sniffing around your equipment. Secondly, leaving sap or moisture on the blades can lead to the formation of rust, creating a habitat for bacteria that will get into future cuttings and can negatively affect the cutting being taken, as well as the mother plant that is being cut. After each use, be sure to wipe your blades with a soft cloth and rubbing alcohol to stop any rust or bacteria building up. Make sure that shears or knives are completely dry before storing in a cool, dry space away from kids or pets. If your tools do develop rust over time, you can scrub it away using lemon juice and salt and wipe the blades with a soft sponge.

WATERING CAN

There is a saying that many in the plant-loving community like to use: "You can never have too many plants." While I love the idea of that, I don't believe it to be true. I've met plenty of people that had too many plants—I could tell because some of their plants were suffering. When it gets to that level, you need to be honest with yourself and admit that you have too many plants to care for properly.

So I have a saying of my own that sounds better: "You can never have too many watering cans." It's true! If, like me, you love creating lush environments, you'll no doubt have a go-to watering can at home. In fact, you'll probably have a whole collection of stylish watering cans that are perfect for keeping all your plant babies hydrated and happy.

My excuse is that when it comes to watering cans, one size does not fit all. You see, some propagation vessels have large openings wherein any size nozzle will be sufficient, while smaller vessels will require a long, thin spout. When attempting to top up the water level of a cutting in a test tube, a watering can with a large spout would be overkill, creating spillage and an unnecessary mess. Having the right-size spout will keep your space clean and help prevent any moisture damage that might take place due to water spilling onto surfaces in your home.

VESSELS

Making sure you have the right vessels for propagation is key to successful root development. Your vessel could be made from various materials—plastic, metal, terra-cotta, ceramic, and so on—but my preference is always for glass. The reason being that glass vessels allow more light to reach the cutting, increasing the chances of healthy root growth.

Glass vessels come in all different colors—amber from a vintage pharmacy bottle, green from a

repurposed wine bottle, or the clear glass of a new vase. My choice would be the latter. Yes, I do use different-colored glass vessels to propagate my plants, but if I were to take a cutting from one of the rarest and most precious plants in the world, and it was my responsibility to propagate it, I would put my faith in a clear glass vessel. It not only allows more light to reach the roots, but it also makes it easier for you to see when the water is starting to become murky and bacteria is building up, giving you a clear signal that it needs to be refreshed.

Colored-glass vessels are still a good choice for propagating because they'll allow more light in than a solid container. However, it won't be as easy to gauge when the water has turned murky. And a solid vessel, like a ceramic or porcelain vase, may look very stylish in your home, but it is likely that a cutting's root development will take longer and require you to check in more often to makes sure all is well.

PLANTER

Once a fine root system has developed, you'll be ready to transition your cutting into soil (see pages 124–137). This is the home where your cutting will grow and mature. The staple planter in the propagation process is a plastic nursery pot. Luckily, anyone who has built a plant family, or has a slight obsession with purchasing new plants, will find themselves with an abundance of such pots. Of course, these can be recycled or returned to your local nursery, but if you love to propagate, hang on to a stack of them, because they come in very useful for cuttings.

PROP LIKE A PRO
These tools of the trade will have you propagating like a pro in no time (opposite and above). When in doubt, I always default to water propagation; however, it doesn't hurt to have some spare pots at hand.

A CUT ABOVE THE REST

A REASON FOR THE SEASON

There are many reasons you might want to propagate a plant and perhaps the most typical is to add to your collection. While plant shopping for the plant lover can be a sort of therapy, there is nothing more therapeutic than FREE. Taking a cutting from a plant you already own and propagating it to increase your investment is just too enticing. And when you think of all the plants your friends and family own...well, that small collection of yours can literally grow overnight. When it comes to being a plant parent, going from zero to a hundred plants in a short amount of time is not surprising.

Propagation is also one of the last resorts to save a dying plant by giving it a second chance at life. But that second chance won't come unless the knowledge of how to fully care for the mother plant has been acquired. For this reason, I always say that you need to learn how to care for the plants you have before trying to propagate them and thereby increase your workload and stress levels. One main reason why plant parents might have problems is that they don't have the proper light to allow their plants to thrive. In that situation, propagating may not be enough to save a struggling plant. The best thing to do would be to take the cutting and gift it to someone who has the right light for it to flourish.

A third reason to propagate is as a method of pruning, perhaps if you have a plant that needs to be cut back to prevent it from growing out of control or to give it a more attractive shape. When you trim or shape your plants, instead of discarding the cut ends, consider using them for propagation. Nothing is wasted and you get to grow new plants for your own collection or to gift to loved ones.

The best time of year to propagate is any time between spring and summer. It's when most plants are actively growing and pushing out new life into the world. That's why they call this time of year "grow season." However, regardless of the season, if your plants are actively growing, you can successfully propagate them. When you take cuttings, it can help to encourage new growth on the mother plant. You're not only taking a piece of the plant to create more, but you're encouraging the mother plant to grow larger. This is the process used to encourage a tree to branch out. (Find out more about branching your plant on pages 34–39.)

FRESH CUT
A newly trimmed *Philodendron scandens* 'Brasil' vine (above). This *Pilea peperomioides* leaf cutting has healthy roots and is ready to be planted (opposite). Behind it, a *Peperomia prostrata* cutting cascades down the wall.

LIFE AND DEPTH
Plant cuttings in propagation cradles on my gallery wall (opposite). *Philodendron scandens* 'Brasil' about to be cut (left). Deciding where to make the cut on a ZZ plant (below left). A *Ficus triangularis* styled on a pedestal (below right).

CUTTING IT CLOSE

Before you attempt to operate on your plant friend or plant baby, it's important to understand exactly where to make the cut. While you may have luck developing roots from any cutting you might take, your best shot for success will be to identify a healthy part of the plant that is showing new growth and take a cutting from there. This is the plant's way of telling you that it is capable of pushing out new growth in the future.

All cuttings are not equal. If you are looking to propagate a variegated plant and you identify a particular leaf that you are enamored with and want its particular coloration or markings to be recreated once propagated, you'll have to cut right below that leaf to get the results you desire. Let's say you have a variegated wax plant (*Hoya carnosa* 'Albomarginata') with leaves that are mainly white. If you take a cutting of a white leaf, it is likely that the new growth will resemble that one. But if you took a cutting from a part of the plant that has mainly green leaves, the new growth would more than likely be, well...green.

And it's not just about the color of your chosen leaf—think about its other qualities, too. Let's say you take a cutting from a large Swiss cheese plant (*Monstera deliciosa*) and choose a leaf that has many attractive holes and splits. The new growth from that cutting, when given the right light and cared for properly, will resemble that of the initial leaf. If, on the other hand, you took a cutting from the same plant with no holes or splits, the new growth might develop similar holes and splits over time, but not as quickly as if you had chosen a cutting that already has them. Put simply, cut what you want to create.

STEM CUT

One of the most utilized and best understood methods of propagation is the stem cut method. And when I say "stem," it's exactly that. You're looking to cut the stem of a vine-like plant—monsteras, philodendrons, hoyas, syngoniums, and so on. I know what you're asking yourself. "Does he mean literally any vine plant?" In most cases, the answer is yes. And when you take a cutting from a vine plant, new growth will develop right above the next leaf on the vine. So not only are you taking a cutting to make a new plant, but the mother plant will push out new growth, too.

THE PLANTS

If you're unsure whether your plants can be propagated via this method, search for an indicator on the vine itself. You are looking for some sort of bump, which is called a node. On many vine plants, including monsteras, pothos, or philodendrons, there will be a node below every leaf growth. It may appear as a small bump, or be elongated and look like a long root, in which case it is called an aerial root. (In the wild, vine plants use aerial roots to climb trees and reach up toward the sun.) If you're unable to identify a node, the next-best option would be to make your cut below any leaf growth along the vine.

THE METHOD

Once you have identified where you want to make your cut, take a sharp pair of shears and cut 1–2in/2.5–5cm below the node or leaf growth. This will allow for the cutting to sit easily in any size vessel, or sit deeper into the moss or soil, so that the node is submerged. Don't worry about the direction in which the cut is made, because when propagating a vine plant, roots will develop from either the node or below the leaf of your cutting.

THE DEEP DIVE

The good news is that if a vine of your 'Marble Queen' pothos has 10 leaves, you can potentially create 10 new plants from that single vine. From each single node, once cut and placed either in water, moss or soil, roots may grow. Of course, there is no guarantee that every cutting will succeed, but the likelihood of having a few nodes produce roots is much higher than if you take a chance on a single node. That's why it's important to always cut more than you might need.

If a node fails to produce roots, it will begin to die. You'll be able to tell because the cut end and

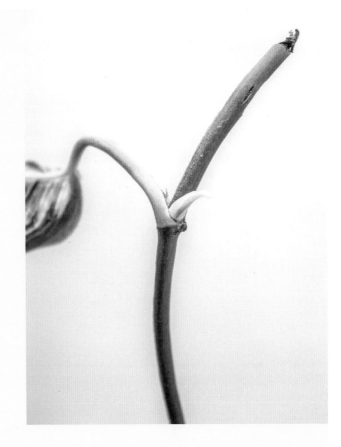

node will turn dark and mushy. If all your hopes were placed on that one single node, you'd be out of luck. But if this were to happen to a cutting that had multiple leaves with multiple nodes, you could simply cut off the dying part and then try again with the next node, and so on. As I like to say, set yourself up for success, but be prepared to make adjustments.

Once you know about a particular plant, not only do you gain understanding of how to care for that one plant but also every other plant in the same family, also known as a genus. This applies to propagation too. Once you understand how to propagate a plant in any given genus, you will also know how to propagate its family members.

A common misconception that plant parents have about taking cuttings from one of their beloved plants is that they are preventing the mother plant from growing or even harming it. Rest assured that isn't the case, as long as the mother plant is thriving.

The following pages cover a few of my favorite plants to propagate via the stem cut method.

PHILODENDRON

The *Philodendron* family includes my favorite types of tropical houseplants and probably my favorite plants in general. Their diversity of appearance makes them all so stunning. For me, any philodendron can transform an indoor space and transport those sitting beside it to that tropical place in their mind that they hope to one day visit, or to visit again. I love the way philodendrons use their aerial roots to lift themselves high above the jungle floor, saying hello to the trees they embrace with care and reaching for the sun that gives them life.

I've propagated my fair share of philodendron plants and have had great success doing so. My collection at home is a direct testament to this. What makes a philodendron an ideal plant to propagate is the fact that its nodes grow larger and are easy to spot, making it straightforward to identify where to make the cut. One useful thing to know about the philodendron plant, or any plant with a node, is that if that node grows longer and becomes an aerial root, you can trim it as desired without harming the plant.

» *Root development should take place in 1–3 weeks.*

A *Philodendron* 'Painted Lady' plant about to be cut below a set of nodes (above from left); after the cut; the cutting submerged in water. *P. scandens* 'Micans' climbing up a wall (left).

HOYA

Like many plants that we bring indoors, the better the quality of light, soil, and fertilizer that they are given, the more likely they are to produce blooms. The *Hoya* family has some of the most beautiful and fragrant blooms of any tropical plant you can grow indoors. I'm putting them up there with orchids, because that's where they deserve to be. Plus, they are much easier to propagate than an orchid, so they get bonus points there.

Unlike other vine-like plants, where you'll see a noticeable node below every single new leaf growth, the nodes of hoyas are found along the entire vine. They are small in stature and can be missed if you're not looking closely. Because there are so many nodes along a vine, you can cut wherever you please, not necessarily focusing on one particular node. Once placed in an appropriate rooting medium, any node that is submerged will begin to produce roots and this is the same for every type of plant in the *Hoya* family.

» *Root development should take place in 2–4 weeks.*

A sun-bleached *Hoya carnosa* vine waiting to be cut (above right). Trailing *Hoya macrophylla* vines (right). A green *Hoya carnosa* in full bloom and climbing up a pendant light (below).

MONSTERA

The *Monstera* family is most widely known for its mascot, the Swiss cheese plant (*Monstera deliciosa*), which can be seen in many tropical destinations, or gracing elegant homes in any interiors magazine. However, there are many other wonderful monsteras to choose from.

One of the most appealing features of monsteras is the way their foliage develops, creating natural holes and splits that allow light and moisture to make their way through the plant. Whether you're into one of the many standard green varieties, or are looking to elevate your collection with one of the dramatic variegated options, you'll be welcoming a statement piece into your home.

Just like the philodendron, the monstera is straightforward to propagate and its long nodes make it easy to identify where to cut. While I've seen plenty of designers and stylists cut large monstera leaves off a mother plant to style in vases like cut flowers, they are often not cut at the right part of the stem for propagation. Knowing exactly where to make the cut will allow cuttings to develop roots and they can then be potted, grow into new plants, and potentially propagated again. This is not the case for leaves cut at the wrong spot, which will die over time.

» *Root development should take place in 1–3 weeks.*

Monstera peru **is beautiful without holes or splits in its leaves (above left).** *Rhaphidophora tetrasperma* **climbing a wall (left). A** *Monstera deliciosa* **'Thai Constellation' stem has its aerial root cut short to fit in a vessel (below from left).**

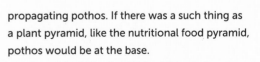

POTHOS

I would be doing everyone a disservice if I didn't speak about the *Pothos* family while discussing the topic of propagation. As you've read earlier in this book, the first plant I ever propagated was a golden pothos (*Epipremnum aureum*), and it was gifted to me by the same individual who taught me how to propagate the plant. I sometimes say the pothos was probably the first plant ever brought into the home and used as decor instead of turning into salad. Think about it—who do you know who has a plant and doesn't have a pothos? Nobody. The reason pothos are so popular is that they're a low-maintenance option. They aren't pushy or demanding, but loving and forgiving.

Pothos are also extremely easy to propagate. One could even say too easy. You could probably just throw a cutting at any root medium and see roots develop in seconds. I'm exaggerating, of course, but it can truly seem that easy. If I were to start a plant business, I would start by propagating pothos. If there was a such thing as a plant pyramid, like the nutritional food pyramid, pothos would be at the base.

» *Root development should take place in 1–3 weeks.*

Silver satin pothos (*Scindapsus pictus* 'Argyraeus') on a concrete wall (above left). Golden pothos showing where it gets its name (top). A 'Shangri La' pothos cutting (above).

5 FAVORITES

TO PROPAGATE USING THE STEM CUT METHOD

1 CISSUS DISCOLOR

I tend to judge whether or not a plant is one of my favorites to propagate based on how likely it is that I'd try to take a cutting of it from a friend. As they say, the heart wants what it wants. And I for one, listen to my heart when I see a *Cissus discolor*, the vine version of *Begonia* Rex Cultorum Group.

While there are plenty of Rex begonias that you could choose to propagate, *Cissus discolor* is by far one of my favorites. It also happens to be one of the more interesting vining plants to style as a cutting. While its unusual colors and texture will probably be the first qualities that jump out at you, I also love how the vines can cascade down a vessel when rooting in water. And as is the case with many vining plants, your chances of seeing your *Cissus discolor* cutting develop roots are extremely high.

» *Root development should take place in 1–3 weeks. When ready to pot, here are some general tips for how to care for the cutting:*

LIGHT Medium light – bright indirect light. No direct sun.

WATER With lukewarm water, to keep the soil moist but not wet. Never let the soil completely dry out. Mist every few days.

TEMPERATURE 60–80°F/16–26°C during the day and no lower than 60°F/16°C at night

SOIL Place in a potting mix that retains a bit of moisture.

REPOTTING Repot in spring or summer. Make sure the new pot is 2in/5cm larger than the previous pot.

PLANTER Best in a glazed ceramic or plastic container that helps retain moisture.

2 PHILODENDRON 'PAINTED LADY'

When it comes to the 'Painted Lady', you'll never find yourself having a hard time gifting a cutting to someone. In fact, your issue will mainly be with trying to hold your friends and family back from stealing a cutting from you. Trust me, I've had that issue myself. The beauty of this plant is undeniable and when seen in someone's home, the desire to have it for your very own is strong. So for you it's a good thing it's fairly easy to propagate. I can't say the same if you're the proprietor of a plant store.

One of the reasons that *Philodendron* 'Painted Lady' is among my favorite plants to propagate is simply because of how easy it is. This in turn makes it easier for me to share. The deciding factor is the number of nodes that grow below each leaf growth. While many vining plants will produce a single node below a leaf growth, the 'Painted Lady' may have two, three, or even four. These extra nodes make the chances of developing roots much higher.

» Root development should take place in 1–3 weeks. When ready to pot, here are some general tips for how to care for the cutting:

LIGHT Bright indirect light – medium light.

WATER With lukewarm water, when the top half of the soil is completely dry, making sure to water until it comes out of the drainage hole of the planter.

TEMPERATURE 65–75°F/18–24°C during the day and no lower than 60°F/16°C at night.

SOIL Place in a potting mix that is free-draining and aerated.

REPOTTING Repot during spring or summer. Make sure the new pot is at least 2in/5cm larger than the previous pot.

PLANTER Best in a porous container made of terra-cotta, ceramic, cement, or clay.

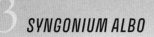

3 SYNGONIUM ALBO

OMG! Yeah, that's exactly what one says when looking at the *Syngonium albo*. Then the next thing you are likely to hear is the blades of a pair of shears opening and then closing. A cutting from the mother plant has been taken. This beautiful vining plant should be shared with as many loved ones as possible. Well, that's if you want to truly show them you care. No pressure, of course. It's your plant and your love, and you can share it however you please. I will say though, it's much easier to give a piece of your syngonium away than a piece of your heart.

Just like all stem-cut plants, you want to identify the node and make the cut below it. With the *Syngonium albo*, there are plenty of nodes to choose from. With variegated plants, the type of leaf you cut will more likely determine the type of new leaf that will eventually grow along that vine. So when taking a cutting from the Albo, pick a leaf that feels exciting to you in order to produce a similar look in the future.

» Root development should take place in 1–3 weeks. When ready to pot, here are some general tips for how to care for the cutting:

LIGHT Medium light – bright indirect light. No direct sun.

WATER With lukewarm water, to keep the soil moist but not wet. Never let the soil completely dry out. Mist every few days.

TEMPERATURE 60–80°F/16–26°C during the day and no lower than 60°F/16°C at night.

SOIL Place in a potting mix that retains a bit of moisture.

REPOTTING Repot during spring or summer. Make sure the new pot is 2in/5cm larger than the previous pot.

PLANTER Best in a glazed ceramic or plastic container that helps retain moisture.

4 PIPER CROCATUM

The *Piper crocatum* had me at hello. Hello, friend! While it is considered a rare houseplant at the moment, after you see it in the wild (i.e. a plant store near you), you'll instantly get to propagating it, again and again, gifting it to friend after friend, and soon, it won't be rare at all. Just another incredible plant for everyone to enjoy. That's my hope at least. I wouldn't want to be one of only a few people who get to enjoy this amazing plant styled in their home.

I love how the crocatum's tortoiseshell design and the silvery sheen of the foliage look against other plants I have in my collection. In fact, I love this plant so much that it inspires me to propagate it often so that I can have its vines dripping throughout my home. That feeling won't escape you as well.

Propagating most pipers is easy. Propagating all pipers is fun! The same goes for the crocatum. While I love seeing them develop roots in water, displayed in my cradle vessels, I've seen them really show off when placed in sphagnum moss, too.

» Root development should take place in 1–3 weeks. When ready to pot, here are some general tips for how to care for the cutting:

LIGHT Medium light – bright indirect light. No direct sun.

WATER With lukewarm water, to keep the soil moist but not wet. Never let the soil completely dry out. Mist every few days.

TEMPERATURE 60–80°F/16–26°C during the day and no lower than 60°F/16°C at night.

SOIL Place in a potting mix that retains a bit of moisture.

REPOTTING Repot during spring and summer. Make sure the new pot is at least 2in/5cm larger than the previous pot.

PLANTER Best in a glazed ceramic or plastic container that helps retain moisture.

5 *MONSTERA DELICIOSA* 'THAI CONSTELLATION'

Some say there is no such thing as too many plants. When it comes to 'Thai Constellation', they might be right. The more, the merrier! This rare, majestic flame of a plant is one that many wish they could add to their collection so they can showcase its beauty in their home. We're all familiar with the *Monstera deliciosa*, and 'Thai Constellation'

looks as though the deliciosa was given to a toddler and they painted it with white paint. That white, its variegated foliage, is what makes it a stunner.

When it comes to propagating a variegated plant like this, many are hoping that they will produce new growth with more white than green. If this is something that's important

to you, take a look at the stem where the node is located and this will give you a good sense of what will unfurl next. If the stem where the node is located has a mix of white and green in it, you're more than likely to see a highly variegated leaf. If the stem where the node is located has more green, the next leaf to unfurl will lean more to the green side. So make the cut wisely. But at the end of the day, no matter what the new growth looks like from your cutting, consider yourself lucky to have one.

» Root development should take place in 1–3 weeks. When ready to pot, here are some general tips for how to care for the cutting:

LIGHT Bright indirect light – medium light.

WATER With lukewarm water, when the top half of the soil is completely dry, making sure to water until it comes out of the drainage hole of the planter.

TEMPERATURE 65–75°F/18–24°C during the day and no lower than 60°F/16°C at night.

SOIL Place in a potting mix that is free-draining and aerated.

REPOTTING Repot during spring or summer. Make sure the new pot is at least 2in/5cm larger than the previous pot.

PLANTER Best in a porous container made of terra-cotta, ceramic, cement, or clay.

TIP
CUT

Knowing how to identify the type of cut that will best help your plant develop roots is everything. Getting this wrong could lead to your cutting dying and even put the mother plant into a downward spiral. Trust me, I know the disappointment of thinking I was taking a proper cutting from my first plant, Frank, my fiddle leaf fig. Not only did the cutting I took from him die, but Frank went into shock and lost a few leaves as a result. So what I always say is to walk through the steps and make sure you've chosen the right method for your particular plant.

THE PLANTS

The tip cut method of propagating is exactly what it sounds like: you're cutting the tip of the plant. If the plant you're looking to propagate has vines or a noticeable node, go with a stem cut, but if not, the next method you're going to look to use is the tip cut. This technique will be used on many tree-like plants, such as ficus trees, dracaenas, scheffleras, money trees, crotons, and aralias. It also works for any plant that has stems but isn't a vine: ZZ plants, cacti, succulents, dieffenbachias, and peperomias.

THE METHOD

With tree plants, the important thing is to identify where on the branch or stem to make the cut for the best results. Look at the base of the branch where it's hard and tree-like, then make your way up that branch toward the newer growth, until you find the spot where it starts to turn a brownish-green color. From that spot, anywhere up to the tip of the branch, is where you'll want to make your cut for the best results. Your success rate here is about 80–95 percent.

For any other plants that aren't trees but don't have vines, you can honestly make the cut wherever you like. For example, if you're taking a cutting from a ZZ plant, the entire stem is green. Wherever on the stem you cut, you have a high likelihood of success.

When making the cut, take a sharp, clean pair of shears and cut the branch or stem at a 45° angle. Once you've made the cut, wipe off any sap from the cutting and from the mother plant. Make sure to check the floor as well—sap from many of these plants can be toxic to humans and pets, so it's important to clean any surfaces that it could have come in contact with. Now that you've made the cut, head over to Chapter 9: Root Development (pages 76–85) to decide what medium you'd like to use to develop the root system.

THE DEEP DIVE

Making an angled cut allows a greater surface area to be exposed to moisture, giving you more room for roots to grow. It also helps in instances where a long cutting touches the base of the vessel. If you were to make a straight cut, the base of the cutting might end up flush against the bottom of the vessel, making it difficult for the cutting to push out roots. An angled cut lifts it up off the bottom, giving it room to push out roots.

Just like vine plants, when taking the cutting from a mother plant using the tip cut method, new growth will develop between where the cut was made and right above the next leaf on the branch or stem. Many use this method to actually encourage their mother plants to branch out. Depending on whether you've made the cut during grow season and the plant is well cared for and in the right light, you could see multiple new branches grow out from the tip cut.

The following pages showcase a few of my favorite plants to propagate via the tip cut method.

FICUS

The first plant I ever owned or loved was a ficus. If you've read my book *Wild at Home*, you'll be aware that it was a *Ficus lyrata*, aka a fiddle leaf fig, that I would eventually name Frank. It was the large, fiddle-like foliage and the tree shape of the lyrata that got me excited to bring it into my home. I think the things that make many of us excited about ficus plants are their tree-like shapes and their ability to grow fairly large indoors. Because of this, they are the most commonly styled statement plants in homes. I mean, who can resist having a tree in their home? An actual tree. I couldn't and still can't. I try to find a spot for a ficus in every space I style and I have many in my own collection, too.

When it comes to propagating ficus plants, they are not the easiest to successfully produce roots or transition into soil. As I mentioned earlier in this chapter, I've had cuttings die on me in the past. Like many plants you look to propagate, it can take some time before you see root development. It just so happens that ficus plants take an extra bit of time. As they say, "Anything worth having is worth waiting for," so stay patient. It's never guaranteed that your cuttings will produce roots or that your cutting will live, but remember, if the foliage is still upright and bright, you're on the right path.

» *Root development should take place in 8–10 weeks.*

A variegated *Ficus benjamina* in the process of being cut (above left). Two recently planted *F. elastica* 'Shivereana' cuttings (left). A happy *F. elastica* unfurling new growth (below).

DRACAENA

There is something so wonderful about seeing a dracaena plant indoors. Regardless of the type of dracaena you have, the way the foliage sits at the tips of their branches like pom-poms shaking in celebration, or fireworks exploding, really brings life into your home. One of the many reasons why I love to style them indoors is the way their thin branches bend and organically stretch out into a room, adding texture and pattern against whatever they stand close to. Since the foliage only tends to sit at the tips of the branches, they can provide a space with life and lushness, without blocking light from reaching other plants and other parts of a room.

Unlike with a ficus or schefflera, where you're looking to make the cut within the part of the branch that is greenish brown or full green in color, on dracaenas, you can take the cut wherever you'd like on the branch, even if it's brown. Dracaenas are on the easier side to propagate when given the right care. I've had the best success taking the cutting and letting it root in water. But as with all tip-cut plants, propagating a dracaena can feel a little like playing the waiting game. So I hope at the end of your wait, you find a win.

» *Root development should take place in 3–5 weeks.*

This Song of India (*Dracaena reflexa*) branch has been cut and then pushed out a new branch (above left). *D. marginata* foliage (above right). *D. reflexa* growing in a pot (right).

PEPEROMIA

If you've ever wondered why plant shops have so many small planters for sale, the short answer is...peperomias. Known for their adorable foliage and candlestick blooms, they are perfect to style on coffee tables, bookshelves, and other small areas of the home. What I absolutely love about peperomia is how low maintenance they are and the many varieties there are to choose from. And who out there doesn't like options? All of this makes them one of my favorite plant genera to add to my collection and, of course, to propagate.

The *Peperomia* family doesn't present itself like your typical tip-cut plant, meaning you aren't looking for where the stems start to turn green because all the stems on a peperomia are green. So when you're ready to propagate one, you can make the cut anywhere on the plant. You can even just take a cut of a single leaf and propagate that. (If you're looking to learn more about the leaf cut method, head to page 45.) When taking a tip cut of a peperomia, it's ideal to cut the stem right above a set of leaf growth so that you have more stem to submerge in your rooting medium. Since peperomia have very thin stems, the cutting may require a smaller vessel to keep it submerged.

» *Root development should take place in 2–4 weeks.*

A *Peperomia tetragona* stretches out its stems to make its presence known (above right). A cutting from the same plant in water (below). The foliage of the watermelon peperomia, *P. argyreia*, reflects its namesake (right).

CACTI

If you're reading this book right now, you're definitely a lover of plants. But I have a question...where are all of my stabby plant lovers? Or in layman's terms...cactus lovers. There is no other family of plants that knows better how to protect itself more than the cactus family. So many varieties, so many knives. But you have to admit, the family of cacti available to bring into your home, to design your own indoor desert, is quite vast. In all honesty, there are probably just as many cacti varieties as there are succulents. But as they say, never bring a succulent to a cactus fight. Or something like that.

If you are a cactus lover, the great thing about them is that they are fairly easy to propagate. While most of your cacti will be green from the tip to the base of the plant, mature specimens can be hard, brown, and tree-like at the base. If this is the case, just like with a ficus, you'll want to avoid making the cut in that area and look to make it wherever the cactus is green. For taking a tip cut of a cactus, a sharp blade is required. Take your knife and make a clean and

sharp angled cut. Then take the cutting and lean it up against a wall or flat surface in your home, making sure the cut end is exposed so that it can dry out and callus over. In terms of light requirements, while it's understandable that you'd want to place it in direct sun, this is not what you should do. The ideal light for a cactus is bright indirect light, just like other propagated plants.

» Once your cutting is callused at the cut end, it should be ready to plant in soil. If you've taken a cutting from a cactus that can be rooted in water, you should see root development in 3–5 weeks.

5 FAVORITES
TO PROPAGATE USING THE TIP CUT METHOD

1 FICUS BENGHALENSIS 'AUDREY'

'Audrey' is an instant standout among many in the *Ficus* family. Unlike some of its cousins, this plant's branches are an elegant shade of gray and smooth to the touch. If you're a fan of the fiddle leaf fig (*Ficus lyrata*) you'll love this ficus. Especially since it's not as finicky (and who doesn't love a plant that already has a name?!).

'Audrey' is one of my favorites to propagate as pruning back the mother plant will encourage it to push out new branches, so I'm not wasting any part of the plant. Plus, it doesn't hurt that 'Audrey' grows so well in any rooting medium she is placed in.

» *Root development should take place in 8–10 weeks. When ready to pot, here are some tips for general care of the cutting:*

LIGHT Bright indirect light – morning direct sunlight.

WATER With lukewarm water when the top half of the soil is completely dry, making sure to water until it comes out of the drainage hole of the planter.

TEMPERATURE 65–80°F/18–26°C during the day and no lower than 60°F/15°C at night.

SOIL Place in a potting mix that is free-draining and aerated.

REPOTTING Repot during spring or summer. Make sure the new pot is at least 2in/5cm larger than the previous pot.

PLANTER Best in a porous container made of terra-cotta, ceramic, cement, or clay.

2 FICUS ELASTICA 'SHIVEREANA'

This plant may not be new to all of you, but I'm sure it's new to many. And when you see it, it will grab you. What I love about this ficus, beyond its incredible speckled foliage, is that it's not as fussy as its cousin the fiddle leaf fig, and will look great nestled up to any other plant you own. If you're looking to bring life and color into a room, 'Shivereana' should be on your wishlist.

As with all ficus plants, the best way to propagate 'Shivereana' is where the stem of the branch changes from brownish green to pure green. While it'll take some time for your cutting to start developing roots, please believe me when I say it'll be time well spent.

» Root development should take place in 8–10 weeks. When ready to pot, here are some tips for general care of the cutting:

LIGHT Bright indirect light – morning direct sunlight.

WATER With lukewarm water, when the top half of the soil is completely dry, making sure to continue until water comes out of the drainage hole of the planter.

TEMPERATURE 65–80°F/18–26°C during the day and no lower than 60°F/15°C at night.

SOIL Place in a potting mix that is free-draining and aerated.

REPOTTING Repot during spring or summer. Make sure the new pot is at least 2in/5cm larger than the previous pot.

PLANTER Best in a porous container made of terra-cotta, ceramic, cement, or clay.

3 POLKA DOT BEGONIA (*BEGONIA MACULATA*)

The polka dot begonia is on my shortlist of "designer" plants. Its patterned foliage is so striking. Then when it gifts you with blooms, it becomes an entirely different kind of party! What more could you ask for in a plant? Maybe for it to be easy to propagate? Well, don't worry—you'll get that with this begonia as well.

The polka dot is a good choice for the tip cut method, because it roots well in most mediums and doesn't have any issues developing new growth. It looks best when there are multiple stalks growing from the pot, so you'll have to propagate a few before your planter looks fully wild.

» Root development should take place in 2–4 weeks. When ready to pot, here are some tips for general care:

LIGHT Medium light – bright indirect light. No direct sun.

WATER Give them a drink with lukewarm water and keep the soil moist but not wet. Never let the soil completely dry out. Mist every few days.

TEMPERATURE 60–80°F/15–26°C during the day, and no lower than 60°F/15°C at night.

SOIL Place in a potting mix that retains moisture.

REPOTTING Repot during spring and summer. Make sure your new pot is at least 2in/5cm larger than the previous pot.

PLANTER Best in a glazed ceramic or plastic container that helps retain moisture.

4 RAVEN ZZ PLANT (*ZAMIOCULCAS ZAMIIFOLIA* 'RAVEN')

Have you ever considered the Raven ZZ? If you haven't, you will now. It has all the wonderful qualities of the green ZZ plant but—get this—in black. And, as the saying goes, the blacker the ZZ plant, the sweeter the juice. What do you mean? Someone definitely said that!

I love ZZ plants because they can be propagated using so many different methods—you can cut a single stem, a leaf, or just separate them at the roots and repot them (see pages 60–61). And the beauty of the Raven ZZ is that it adds an unexpected pop of drama against all the hues of greenery you have in your home.

» Root development should take place in 2–4 weeks. When ready to pot, here are some tips for general care of the cutting:

LIGHT Low light – direct sunlight.

WATER With lukewarm water when the soil is completely dry (every 2–3 weeks) making sure to keep going until water comes out of the drainage hole of the planter.

TEMPERATURE 65–80°F/18–26°C during the day and no lower than 55°F/13°C degrees at night

SOIL Place in a potting mix that is free-draining and aerated.

REPOTTING Repot during spring or summer. Make sure the new pot is at least 2in/5cm larger than the previous pot.

PLANTER Best in a porous container made of terra-cotta, ceramic, cement, or clay.

5 SONG OF INDIA (*DRACAENA REFLEXA*)

OK, hear me out. I know this might sound a little ridiculous, but I've renamed this plant "Song of Hilton." Maybe because I can't stop singing its praises. Not only is it one of my favorite plants to propagate via the tip cut method, but it's also one of my favorite dracaenas. The way the branches bend and curl as they grow is the very definition of "living wild."

Propagating Song of India isn't quite as easy as other dracaenas, but success can be achieved if you are careful. And even if they start to lose a few leaves, these beauties present themselves like miniature palm trees.

» Root development should take place in 3–5 weeks. When ready to pot, here are some tips for general care of the cutting:

LIGHT Bright indirect light – morning direct sunlight.

WATER With lukewarm water when the top half of the soil is completely dry, making sure to keep going until water emerges from the drainage hole of the planter.

TEMPERATURE 65–80°F/18–26°C during the day and no lower than 60°F/15°C at night.

SOIL Place in a potting mix that is free-draining and aerated.

REPOTTING Repot during spring or summer. Make sure the new pot is at least 2in/5cm larger than the previous pot.

PLANTER Best in a porous container made of terra-cotta, ceramic, cement, or clay.

LEAF CUT

When I first learned how to propagate a stem of golden pothos, I was blown away. I started carrying my scissors with me, snipping cuttings from every plant within my reach. I would cut off a leaf and place it in water, expecting it to develop roots. This process had worked with my golden pothos, so why not every other houseplant? I soon realized that leaf cut propagation was more complicated.

THE PLANTS

The leaf cut is the propagation method that is most misunderstood of all. Taking a single leaf from a plant and expecting roots to grow from its end seems pretty reasonable. In fact, this is one of the least-used methods of propagation, because it only results in success with a select handful of plants. These include peperomias, begonias, snake plants, ZZ plants, succulents, and cacti. Yes, these plants can also be propagated via a tip cut, but if you're looking to start small or add a little pop of color to your home, taking single leaves to propagate is a great way to do so.

THE METHOD

Depending on the type of plant, a leaf cut can either be made along the stem of the plant or just below the leaf itself. If you are working with a ZZ plant, a single leaf can be cut and then propagated, while with a peperomia you must make the cut on the stem that the leaf is attached to. The success rate here is about 80–95 percent (I would say 99 percent, but there is always a chance of human error).

Just as with the tip cut method of propagation (see page 35), you should cut with a clean 45° angle, either cutting the stem of the leaf or the leaf itself, both to create more surface area for roots to develop and to allow the end of the cutting to hover above the bottom of the vessel.

THE DEEP DIVE

After the success I had with my pothos, it was as if I had learned an amazing magic trick and I just had to share it with the world. I would see a vibrantly colored *Stromanthe sanguinea* 'Triostar' at a friend's house and think to myself, "I need to have this plant in my life." And out would come the scissors.

What I didn't realize at the time is that it was sheer good luck that I had chosen a pothos as my first

plant to propagate. On that plant, every leaf has a node that will sprout roots when placed in water, leading me to believe that I would enjoy the same success with other plants. However, many plants aren't that easy to propagate, and it's essential to know exactly where to make the cut. On a different plant, I could easily have cut a stem of a leaf without a node and watched my cutting slowly die in water without ever developing roots. In fact, many have had this experience. But while the stem cut and tip cut are my go-to methods nowadays, leaf cut propagation is perfectly possible to achieve as long as it is done correctly.

Bear in mind that if you remove a single leaf from your plant, a new leaf will not grow in exactly that spot to replace the one you took. That's just something to remember when you are cutting a leaf from a plant—I wouldn't want you to give your plant friend a weird or unbalanced look.

The following pages show a few of my favorite plants to propagate via the leaf cut method.

SUCCULENTS

While these plants can be propagated via the tip cut method (see pages 34–43), you may have a good reason for using the leaf cut over the tip. When repotting a succulent, a few healthy leaves may fall off, and many people just toss these into the trash. In fact, they offer an opportunity to turn trash into treasure in the shape of a whole new plant.

One of the best parts about propagating a succulent via the leaf cut is that you don't have to put in much effort. You may have seen the process take place by accident when a succulent leaf falls onto the soil in the pot of the mother plant. While caring for that mother plant, you are in turn caring for and providing the single leaf with what it needs to push out roots and develop new growth. And by "needs," I'm referring to soil, water, and, of course, light. The process is very simple.

A sandy potting mix is leveled out to receive succulent leaf cuttings (above right). Removing ghost plant leaves to propagate them (below).

YOU WILL NEED
» A flourishing succulent—here I'm using a ghost plant, or *Graptopetalum paraguayense*
» Wide, shallow planter with a drainage hole
» Free-draining potting mix
» Small-nozzle watering can

1 Take a few healthy whole succulent leaves. By healthy, I mean leaves that are plump and bright with color, not soft, mushy, or withered. If they are still attached to the plant, gently twist them until they come away easily.

2 Fill a wide, shallow planter with a coarse, free-draining potting mix that's suitable for succulents (see page 129), leaving the top 10 percent of the pot soil-free.

3 Place the succulent leaves on top of the soil at regular intervals, making sure they are at least 1in/2.5cm apart.

4 With a small-nozzle watering can, slowly pour water over the leaves and soil, until water comes out of the drainage hole in the bottom of the planter. Repeat this step twice a week.

5 Find a spot in your home that gets bright indirect light and place your planter there.

6 After a couple of weeks, you'll see little roots starting to sprout from the cut end of the leaves. These roots will find their way down into the soil, where they begin to develop a strong root system. Once the roots have emerged, water them occasionally, waiting until the soil has completely dried out before watering them again.

7 You should start to see a baby succulent plant, or "pup," develop from the cut end of each of the leaves after 4 to 5 weeks. As the new succulent pup grows, the mother leaf will start to shrivel up and die back. Leave it until it falls away naturally.

Over time, your succulent will grow into a larger plant just like the mother plant you cut it from. Take care of it in the same fashion and you'll be able to propagate it again and again to create more life and grow your collection.

» Root development should take place in 2–4 weeks.

BEGONIA

The begonia movement is upon us. OK, maybe it's not a "movement" per se, but this family of plants is definitely having its moment in the sun. And that's important, because begonias definitely need light. There are many different varieties with attractively shaped and patterned leaves, so wanting more of them in your collection makes sense. And what better way to increase your begonia gang than to propagate the ones you already have?

While you can propagate a begonia using the tip cut method, you can also do so via leaf cut; and in two different ways. Firstly, by cutting a single leaf and placing the stem in water to develop roots, and secondly (and this is the fun way) by making cuts in a leaf, placing it on top of soil to develop roots, and watching it slowly produce new growth. Here's how to propagate a Rex begonia (*Begonia* Rex Cultorum Group) from a leaf cutting.

A Rex begonia leaf being cut with a blade to create a spot for new growth to develop (above right). Cutting a leaf from the mother plant for propagation (below).

YOU WILL NEED
» **Sharp pair of shears/cutting tool**
» **Sharp blade or knife**
» **Large sealable plastic container**
» **Seed potting mix**
» **Sphagnum moss**
» **Water**
» **Plastic pot**

1 Cut a healthy, fully grown leaf from the begonia. Then trim away the stem so that you are left with the leaf alone.

2 Place the leaf upside down on a surface suitable for using sharp tools. Take a sharp blade and make ½in/1cm cuts across the largest veins of the leaf. The new begonia shoots will grow from these cuts.

3 Remove the lid of your plastic container and fill the bottom half with two parts potting mix and one part moss. Mix the two together then water the soil mixture until it's damp and moist but not saturated and wet.

4 Place the begonia leaf on top of the soil with the right side up, gently pressing it down against the soil.

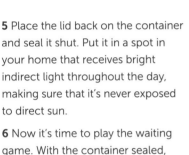

5 Place the lid back on the container and seal it shut. Put it in a spot in your home that receives bright indirect light throughout the day, making sure that it's never exposed to direct sun.

6 Now it's time to play the waiting game. With the container sealed, condensation will build up, bead at the top, and drain back into the soil to keep it moist. This means you won't have to take off the lid to add water. While the leaf should stay happy for most of the process, don't be alarmed if you notice brown spots starting to develop. Remember, it's the new growth that you are waiting for, and the mother leaf will die back while supporting its new pups with nutrients.

7 After about 8 weeks, you should see signs of new life and by 16 weeks you should be able to pot your begonia pups. Gently remove them from the mother leaf by either pulling them off or cutting them away. You should now be able to see their small root systems.

8 Find a plastic pot that is 2in/5cm larger in diameter than the root system to plant the pups in. Using a small spade, scoop some soil from the plastic container into the pot, filling the bottom third. Place the plants in the pot, covering the roots and stems with more soil and pressing down gently to secure them in place. Put your new begonia plants in bright indirect light and keep them evenly moist.

SNAKE PLANT (SANSEVIERIA)

The snake plant gets its name from its attractive scale-like pattern and is a popular and easily available houseplant. Although it's known by most as a "hard to kill" or "office" plant, I have to admit that I killed a few off in my early days. When you're a new plant parent, you tend to smother your plants with love, just like any new parent does. In my case, I gave those poor plants way too much water, but I soon learned my lesson. What I absolutely love about this plant is that, unlike other desert plants, it can be tucked into low-light spots, making it easier to spread the plant love throughout your space even if you don't have huge windows.

One of the wildest ways you can propagate a snake plant is by using the leaf cut method. That's right—you can cut a single leaf and watch as it grows roots and then new shoots. While you can root them in moss or soil, I like to put them in water so that I can watch the shoots develop and grow. If you want to do this too, make sure to place them in a vessel that is twice as wide as the leaf itself. This will give the new shoots room to grow and thrive.

» *Root development should take place in 3–5 weeks, but you'll want to wait until your leaf puts out new shoots before making a transition into soil. These should develop in 8–10 weeks.*

A *Sansevieria zeylanica* about to be cut (above left). The glory of *S. trifasciata* var. *laurentii* (left). Leaf cuttings of *S. zeylanica* and *S. trifasciata* 'Bantel's Sensation' (below).

ZZ PLANT (*ZAMIOCULCAS ZAMIIFOLIA*)

What's great about *Zamioculcas zamiifolia*, or the ZZ plant, is that not only does it have attractively lush, glossy foliage but it is also fairly low maintenance. The ability of ZZ plants to tolerate drought and low light levels makes them the perfect choice for a novice plant parent. And, even better, they're pretty straightforward to propagate.

When it comes to propagating the ZZ, you can either do it via tip cut, division, or, of course, leaf cut. The good thing about using the leaf cut method when propagating a ZZ is that you can create many new plants from a single stem. Each and every leaf has the potential to grow into a new plant, throwing out even more of those exotic, glossy leaves.

Cut the leaves off as close to the stalk as possible, so you have a little part of the stem attached to each cutting. Fill a small, narrow-necked vessel with lukewarm water and push in a leaf, so the end with the stem is below the surface of the water. Place in a warm location with bright indirect light. You will know that propagation has been successful when you see the tip of the leaf starting to develop a tiny round bulb, called a rhizome. Allow the rhizome to grow a little larger before moving it into soil.

» *Root development should take place in 2–4 weeks, with the rhizome developing shortly after.*

A ZZ plant leaf about to be cut ready for propagation (above from left); a leaf cutting placed in water; a leaf that has developed roots after sitting in water for 4 weeks.

5 FAVORITES
TO PROPAGATE USING THE LEAF CUT METHOD

1 FISHBONE CACTUS (*EPIPHYLLUM ANGULIGER*)

Whether you call it the fishbone or sawtooth cactus, this plant is still going to be one of my favorite hanging cacti to bring indoors because it won't stab you if you try to give it a hug and it is also very cooperative when propagated and styled in water. Yes, I understand the confusion around how a cactus that doesn't like to be overwatered can thrive and grow roots when propagated in water. I get it. But trust me, it works. The wild thing about fishbone cactus is that it's an epiphyte, meaning it grows on other trees in nature. So when you style a cutting in a vessel on a wall, it's as if you're mimicking its natural habitat.

LIGHT Bright indirect light – morning direct sunlight.

WATER With lukewarm water, when the top half of soil is completely dry, making sure to water until it comes out of the drainage hole of the planter.

TEMPERATURE 65–80°F/18–26°C during the day and no lower than 60°F/15°C at night.

SOIL Place in a potting mix that is free-draining and aerated.

REPOTTING Repot during spring or summer. Make sure the new pot is at least 2in/5cm larger than the previous pot.

PLANTER Best in a porous container made of terra-cotta, ceramic, cement, or clay.

2 WATERMELON PEPEROMIA (*PEPEROMIA ARGYREIA*)

The watermelon peperomia is one of my favorite plants to have in my home because of how fun the foliage is and how easy it is to propagate. It's probably the number one plant that I propagate and share with others. Being able to just take a quick cut of a leaf, and gift it to someone you love, is very convenient. Plus, when anyone sees the leaf of the watermelon peperomia, they just become so excited. While I wouldn't necessarily call peperomias high maintenance, they do require a lot of moisture and indirect light to thrive indoors. But when you take a single leaf cutting and place it in a vessel, I've seen them thrive in water for extended periods of time before being planted in soil. This makes them such a great plant to be styled as a propagation.

LIGHT Medium light – bright indirect light. No direct sun.

WATER With lukewarm water, to keep the soil moist but not wet. Never let the soil completely dry out. Mist every few days.

TEMPERATURE 60–80°F/15–26°C during the day and no lower than 60°F/15°C at night.

SOIL Place in a potting mix that retains moisture.

REPOTTING Repot during spring or summer. Make sure the new pot is at least 2in/5cm larger than the previous pot.

PLANTER Best in a glazed ceramic or plastic container that helps retain moisture.

3 *BEGONIA* '*BLACK VELVET*'

I'm sure when they said, "Save that drama for your momma," they were talking about the 'Black Velvet' begonia. The drama that its dark foliage can add to a space is just delicious. So yes, save some for your momma and some for yourself, of course. And that's an easy task to accomplish when you can just take a snip of a single leaf, place it in water, and watch it develop roots. When it comes to propagating a plant, there may be times when you're unsure if you should take cuttings because you don't want to make the plant feel unbalanced or bare. But with the 'Black Velvet' begonia growing in a bush-like shape, producing a vast amount of foliage, it doesn't really alter the look of the mother plant if you take a few cuttings here and there, so feel free to get dramatic.

LIGHT Medium light – bright indirect light. No direct sun.

WATER With lukewarm water, to keep the soil moist but not wet. Never let the soil completely dry out. Mist every few days.

TEMPERATURE 60–80°F/15–26°C during the day and no lower than 60°F/15°C at night.

SOIL Place in a potting mix that retains moisture.

REPOTTING Repot during spring or summer. Make sure the new pot is 2in/5cm larger than the previous pot.

PLANTER Best in a glazed ceramic or plastic container that helps retain moisture.

4 SAYURI SNAKE PLANT (*SANSEVIERIA* 'SAYURI')

Sansevieria 'Sayuri' is one of the most elegant members of the snake plant family. Its vertical streaks of soft pale green and white can really create a statement in a room. Unlike the others here that I've pointed out as my some of my favorites, the 'Sayuri', and quite frankly all snake plants, can be difficult to propagate via leaf cut. But what's great about them is that even if the cut end that's placed in water becomes soft and mushy, and it looks as if your cutting is on the path to death, you can cut away the dying part of the leaf and start afresh. That's right, anywhere along the leaf can be cut and produce new shoots. So while this is true of any snake plant, I think the 'Sayuri' is one that should feature in more homes and be added to more plant collections.

LIGHT Low light – direct sunlight.

WATER With lukewarm water, when the soil is completely dry (every 2–3 weeks), making sure to water until it comes out of the drainage hole of the planter.

TEMPERATURE 65–80°F/18–26°C during the day and no lower than 60°F/15°C at night.

SOIL Place in a potting mix that is free-draining and aerated.

REPOTTING Repot during spring or summer. Make sure the new pot is at least 2in/5cm larger than the previous pot.

PLANTER Best in a porous container made of terra-cotta, ceramic, cement, or clay.

5 JADE PLANT (CRASSULA OVATA)

Known for its plump, teardrop-shaped foliage and light brown branches, the jade plant is one of the most common houseplants out there. It's also one of the most frequently propagated plants. This is because, like many succulents, it'll drop its leaves and propagate itself. Yes, you heard me correctly, it propagates itself. So I find it exciting to remove a healthy leaf from my jade plant and lay it on top of the soil in the same pot and watch over time as it develops roots and begins to grow a new little jade. It's a fun and easy way to propagate while still caring for the mother plant.

LIGHT Bright indirect light – direct sunlight.

WATER With lukewarm water, water when the soil is completely dry, making sure to water until it comes out of the drainage hole of the planter.

TEMPERATURE 65–80°F/18–26°C during the day and no lower than 60°F/15°C at night.

SOIL Place in a potting mix that is free-draining and aerated.

REPOTTING Repot during spring or summer. Make sure the new pot is at least 2in/5cm larger than the previous pot.

PLANTER Best in a porous container made of terra-cotta, ceramic, cement, or clay.

DIVISION AND SEPARATION

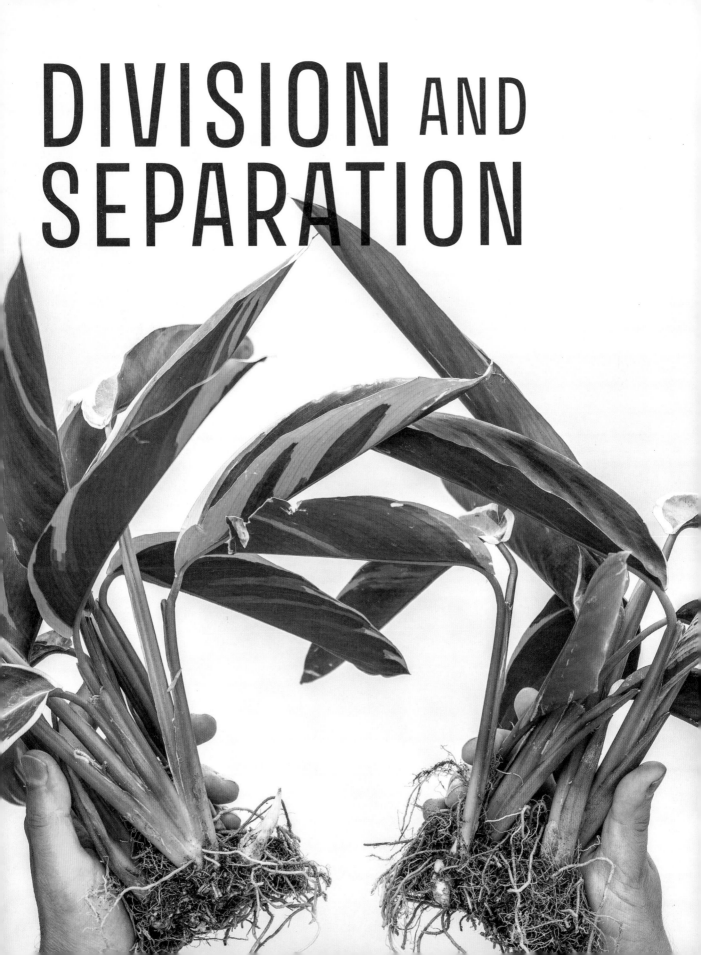

DIVIDE AND CONQUER

What if I were to tell you that not all propagation methods involve taking a sharp blade, cutting off a piece of the mother plant, and then sticking it into a rooting medium? Would you believe me if I promised that you could just divide and separate a plant into sections, immediately increasing the number of plants that you have and, in that way, propagating them?

Well, believe it or not, division and separation, or as I like to call it, "divide and conquer," is one of the most commonly utilized methods of propagation. Despite this fact, many people don't think of it as such, perhaps because it feels more like repotting an existing plant that has outgrown its container. The methods we've discussed on the previous pages all involve taking a cutting from a plant and following certain steps that (hopefully) result in that cutting developing roots so it can be potted in soil. When it comes to division and separation, the plant that you are propagating already has an established root system, making the process of propagation instantaneous.

There are a few reasons why you might want to use this method of propagation. First of all, to increase the number of plants you have in your collection. Secondly, to create room in a pot that is becoming overcrowded. As a plant matures, more shoots develop and grow, leading to competition for light and water because of the lack of sufficient space. Thirdly, you might turn to division and separation to save part of a plant that is healthy but surrounded by other shoots that aren't doing so well.

Most houseplants can be propagated via division and separation, but as with other methods, there is no guarantee of success. The plants that you're likely to have the best success propagating using this method are ferns, bromeliads, caladiums, alocasias, palms, goeppertias and calatheas, and air plants (*Tillandsia*). The process is very similar to repotting a plant and, just as with repotting, it's best to wait until the soil of your plant is on the drier side. Here's how to propagate using division and separation.

BREAK IT UP

Taking a *Stromanthe sanguinea* 'Triostar' from its pot (above). Brushing away the soil (opposite, clockwise from above left); making a cut to the roots; taking the newly separated cutting; planting it into a smaller nursery pot so it can become its own plant.

YOU WILL NEED

» A healthy, mature plant that's outgrowing its current pot
» Sharp pair of shears/cutting tool
» Seed potting mix
» Small spade or trowel
» Smaller pots for the newly divided plants

1 If your plant is in a plastic pot, squeeze the sides to loosen the soil and roots. If your plant is potted in a planter made from a hard material, use a spade or trowel to pull the soil away from the sides of the pot. Firmly hold a portion of your plant at its base and begin to gently work it out of the pot.

2 Once the plant is removed from its pot, use your hands to loosen the soil around the roots. The goal here

is to expose as much of the root system as possible so that you can separate the shoots of the plant.

3 Gently untangle the root system of each shoot. Plant roots can become intertwined, making it difficult to separate them. Don't panic if a few roots snap in the process. You may even have to take a pair of shears or a knife and cut parts of the root system to separate one shoot from another.

4 Each separated section should have a healthy amount of roots, shoots, and leaves.

5 Now that the shoots are separated, the rest of the process is just like repotting a plant. Find a pot that is 2in/5cm larger in diameter than the root system of your shoot and fill the bottom third with potting mix.

6 Gently place a section of the divided plant in the pot, then cover the roots with more soil, patting it firmly into place and leaving the top 10 percent of the pot free of soil. Repeat with the other sections. Water them and place in a warm location with bright indirect light.

You have now successfully propagated your plant via the division and separation method. Caring for these plants shouldn't be new to you, but be aware that their watering needs will be more frequent now that they are in smaller pots with less soil.

The following pages feature a few families of plants that are simple to propagate via the division and separation method.

ALOCASIAS

A question that needs to be asked, and I'm sure many of you will understand me here, is "Why are the most beautiful plants the most problematic to care for?" As someone who is writing a book about propagating plants and rates himself pretty highly in terms of plant parenting, I have to be transparent with you—I have a difficult time with alocasias. They tend to cause me the most stress of all the plants I own, but I can't quit them. I won't. I'd rather be sad with them than happy without them. Maybe it's not that serious, but you understand what I'm trying to say. With alocasias, I often have to propagate them via division and separation in order to preserve those shoots that are doing better than others.

When propagating an alocasia, you'll notice that all its growth is produced at the top of the soil. In many cases, when you first purchase an alocasia it will only have one shoot coming up out of the soil. But as the plant grows and matures, new shoots will break through the top of the soil, and once they get to about half the size of the first shoot, they can be separated and propagated on their own.

The leaves of *Alocasia cuprea* have a glossy pinot-noir underbelly (above left). 'Silver Dragon' has a two-tone coloration with dark green veins (above). Shapely *A. nebula* has silvery foliage (left).

PALMS

Nothing says "tropical" better than a palm tree. When I think of the word, I imagine sitting beneath a canopy of palm fronds, my feet in warm sand and my hand holding a cold beverage. Palms instantly take you to a place of calm and relaxation, so it makes sense that you'd want to have as many as possible surrounding you at home. The only issue is that not every home has the right amount of light and humidity necessary to keep them happy. But if you do, you'll see them grow and produce new shoots from the soil, creating an opportunity for you to propagate them by division.

Palm plants produce new growth at the root level and when that new shoot emerges from the soil, you know you're doing something right. Be patient and let that new shoot develop until it's half the size of the other shoots in the pot before you decide to separate it from the mother plant. This will help it grow its own strong root system before it has to stand alone. In most situations, separating the roots will require cutting them with a blade or shears.

A spindle palm (*Hyophorbe verschaffeltii*) is getting lots of indirect light and air from an open window (above right and below). A pygmy date palm (*Phoenix roebelenii*) sits in the center of the room, adding an elegant tropical feel (right).

GOEPPERTIA

You may not recognize the name of this family of plants, some of which used to be known as calatheas, but they have an incredible wow factor that is alluring to plant parents. While there are a wide variety of goeppertias, every single one is gorgeous. It's the wild pattern on the top of their foliage combined with the vibrant color of the underside of the leaf that gets plant parents all excited and makes us shout, "Take my money!" I, too, have fallen prey to the whims of goeppertias but have learned how to save myself some green, while creating some green (this reference probably doesn't make any sense outside the US, but hopefully you get it!). And the way I've gone about that, my friends, is by propagating them.

You won't have much success cutting off a random goeppertia leaf and placing it in water or adding rooting hormone and placing it directly in soil. Propagating these plants is done using division and separation. You have to separate the clump of shoots at the roots and place each division in a new pot. It sounds fairly simple because it is. It's how you care for each little plant once it's placed in its new home that will make all the difference.

Goeppertia roseopicta showing off its vivid colors (above right). *G. setosa* looks its best in a neutral pot with a plain backdrop that sets off its beauty (right). *G. makoyana* in all its glory (below).

This air plant has three clusters of growth, which can be propagated by removing the pups (above left). I have just pinched off one of them (above).

AIR PLANTS

There aren't many plants as versatile and unique as the *Tillandsia* genus or, as they are better known, air plants. Like staghorn ferns (*Platycerium bifurcatum*) and most orchids, air plants are epiphytes, which means they are plants that grow on other plants, like a host. In their natural habitats, you'll find them clinging to shrubs, bushes, and trees. Because they don't require soil to grow, air plants can be displayed almost anywhere in the home—you just need to find the right light in order for them to flourish. Air plants thrive in bright indirect light, and when given that they will not only show off by growing larger and pushing out blooms but also grow new shoots.

While you can't propagate an air plant by cutting a piece of it and sticking it in a rooting medium to grow roots, what you can do is wait patiently for a mother air plant to grow a new smaller plant, also called a pup, on her side. Once this is at least a third of the size of the mother plant, it can be separated from the mother by gently pulling at its base until it comes away in your hand. If you then provide the pup with the same care that you have been giving its mother, it will grow large, mature, and hopefully grow lots of little pups of its own.

5 FAVORITES
TO PROPAGATE USING DIVISION AND SEPARATION

1 PRAYER PLANT (*GOEPPERTIA ORBIFOLIA*)

I have so much love for tropical plants and the way they can transform a home, and this Bolivian beauty is the perfect example. With its oversized paddle-shaped foliage and dramatic stripes, the prayer plant (formerly known as *Calathea orbifolia*) is an instant standout among its goeppertia cousins. I won't deny that it can be a bit of a diva, as those of you who have grown and killed a few in the past can attest. However, when placed in an environment that mimics its natural habitat in the tropical rainforests of South America, it will grow large and healthy and throw out new shoots. These can be propagated via division and separation to create new plants

LIGHT Medium light – bright indirect light. No direct sun.

WATER With lukewarm water to keep the soil moist but not wet. Never let the soil completely dry out. This plant loves humidity, so mist every few days.

TEMPERATURE 65–80°F/18–26°C during the day and no lower than 60°F/15°C at night.

SOIL Place in a potting mix that retains moisture.

REPOTTING Repot during spring and summer. Make sure the new pot is at least 2in/5cm larger than the previous pot.

PLANTER Best in a glazed ceramic or plastic container that will retain moisture.

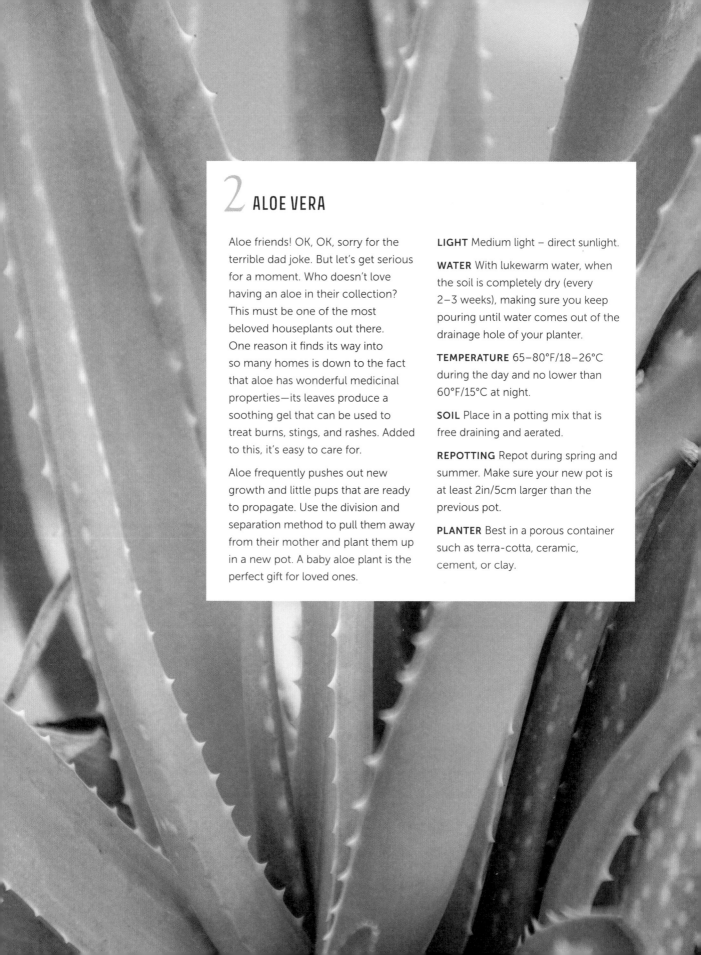

2 ALOE VERA

Aloe friends! OK, OK, sorry for the terrible dad joke. But let's get serious for a moment. Who doesn't love having an aloe in their collection? This must be one of the most beloved houseplants out there. One reason it finds its way into so many homes is down to the fact that aloe has wonderful medicinal properties—its leaves produce a soothing gel that can be used to treat burns, stings, and rashes. Added to this, it's easy to care for.

Aloe frequently pushes out new growth and little pups that are ready to propagate. Use the division and separation method to pull them away from their mother and plant them up in a new pot. A baby aloe plant is the perfect gift for loved ones.

LIGHT Medium light – direct sunlight.

WATER With lukewarm water, when the soil is completely dry (every 2–3 weeks), making sure you keep pouring until water comes out of the drainage hole of your planter.

TEMPERATURE 65–80°F/18–26°C during the day and no lower than 60°F/15°C at night.

SOIL Place in a potting mix that is free draining and aerated.

REPOTTING Repot during spring and summer. Make sure your new pot is at least 2in/5cm larger than the previous pot.

PLANTER Best in a porous container such as terra-cotta, ceramic, cement, or clay.

4 DELTA MAIDENHAIR FERN (*ADIANTUM RADDIANUM*)

There's no denying that it can be difficult to keep a maidenhair fern alive, but with their delicate, lacy foliage they are so beautiful that it's hard to give up on one. I've even killed a few myself. As with most ferns, it will demand the right type of light and, always, the right amount of moisture. Moisture, moisture, moisture! Get that right, and you'll see your maidenhair thrive.

When it comes to propagating maidenhair ferns, the division and separation method is ideal. With so much growth being thrown out by this graceful beauty, you should have plenty of shoots to choose from.

3 CALADIUM LINDENII 'MAGNIFICUM'

'Magnificum' is exactly the right name for this plant. Because this caladium is exactly that—magnificent! Its arrowhead-shaped leaves and unusual markings make it one of my favorite houseplants.

Caladiums require lots of moisture, so they do tend to be at the high-maintenance end of the plant care spectrum, but they are worth it. When your friends and family set eyes on this beauty, they will be green with envy. Thankfully, a thriving 'Magnificum' can push out many new shoots, and division is the best way to share them with all your plant friends.

LIGHT Medium light – bright indirect light. No direct sun.

WATER With lukewarm water, to keep the soil moist but not wet. Never let the soil completely dry out. Mist every few days.

TEMPERATURE 60–80°F/15–26°C during the day, and no lower than 60°F/15°C at night.

SOIL Place in a potting mix that retains moisture.

REPOTTING Repot during spring or summer. Make sure the new pot is at least 2in/5cm larger than the previous pot.

PLANTER Best in a glazed ceramic or plastic container that will retain moisture.

LIGHT Medium light – bright indirect light. No direct sun.

WATER With lukewarm water, to keep the soil moist but not wet. Never let the soil completely dry out. Mist every few days.

TEMPERATURE 60–80°F/15–26°C during the day and no lower than 60°F/15°C at night.

SOIL Place in a potting mix that retains moisture.

REPOTTING Repot during spring or summer. Make sure the new pot is at least 2in/5cm larger than the previous pot.

PLANTER Best in a glazed ceramic or plastic container that will retain moisture.

5 BAMBOO PALM (*RHAPIS EXCELSA*)

What excites me about the bamboo palm (also known as the lady palm) is that you don't tend to see it styled in the home as much as some other palms. Not because it's an unattractive plant, but because it's a little harder to source. So if you are attracted to rare or uncommon species, *Rhapis excelsa* may be the plant for you.

Like many true palms, it can grow to great heights indoors—up to 13ft/4m tall. This creates a jungly mood that will make any space feel like a tropical getaway.

These plants have a tendency to become rootbound quickly, so division and separation is an excellent way to propagate them and prevent overcrowding. Besides, I always think there's something really nice about seeing a single elegant palm growing from a pot.

LIGHT Medium light – morning direct sunlight.

WATER With lukewarm water, when the top half of the soil is completely dry, making sure to continue until water pours out of the drainage hole of the planter.

TEMPERATURE 65–80°F/ 18–26°C during the day and no lower than 60°F/15°C at night.

SOIL Choose a potting mix that is free-draining and aerated.

REPOTTING Repot during spring or summer. Make sure your new pot is at least 2in/5cm larger than the previous pot.

PLANTER Best in a porous container such as terra-cotta, ceramic, cement, or clay.

A
GOOD
SEED

STARTING THE CYCLE

The concept of producing new plants from seeds goes back hundreds of millions of years. It brings to mind the saying, "What came first, the chicken or the egg?", but in this case, it's the plant or the seed. Well, just as the egg came before the chicken, you might assume that the seed came before the plant. That's not strictly true, but at least that's how I make it make sense, and I'll leave the deep dive to the botanists out there. All you need to know is this: the seed produces a plant. The plant produces a flower. The flower is pollinated and then produces fruit, which has seeds (or the flower itself contains the seeds). The fruit and seeds are then taken by gravity, or the wind, or water, or by animals that consume them, and transported to a new location favorable to growth. Then the long, beautiful, and fascinating process starts all over again.

When propagating at home, using a seed, like those taken from the flower of an anthurium or peace lily (*Spathiphyllum wallisii*), or from spores on the underbellies of fern leaves, is rarely the method utilized. Mainly because it's a long and often complicated process, but also because the results aren't always gratifying. However, there is one particular plant that is propagated from seeds across the globe, and that is the avocado plant.

If you eat avocados as often as I do, you'll end up with many avocado seeds, or pits, as we call them, to either dispose of or propagate. If you choose the latter, the avocado seed takes time to produce results, but that process is a beautiful thing to behold. So if you find yourself with an abundance of avocado pits, here is how you can go about propagating your very own avocado plant.

THE PIT

I'm using a spoon to gently scoop out the pit from an avocado in order to propagate it. After removing the pit, I clean it, then insert three toothpicks around the circumference, pushing them in about ½in/1cm (below, left to right).

YOU WILL NEED

» A fresh avocado
» Sharp kitchen knife
» Spoon
» 3–4 wooden toothpicks
» A small glass vessel with a mouth wide enough to sit the seed on
» Fresh water

1 Take a sharp knife and carefully cut your avocado in half, making sure not to slice into the pit.

2 Take the spoon and remove the pit. Rinse off any avocado flesh that is stuck to the pit, then dry it off with a paper towel or cloth.

3 Some plant parents remove the outer brown skin on the pit at this stage to speed up the germination process, but it's not necessary. Take a toothpick and push it into one side of the pit, working closer to its broader, slightly flatter end.

4 Working at regular intervals, push in the other toothpicks. Once they're all in place, you're going to use them to suspend the pit from a small glass jar or vase so that the lower part of the pit is submerged in water.

5 Fill the glass vessel with lukewarm water and place the avocado pit on top. The toothpicks should just allow the bottom half to rest in the water.

6 Place the pit in a spot in your home that receives lots of light and humidity—this is why you'll see many avocado propagations taking place on kitchen windowsills.

7 Now you're going to play a waiting game, checking every few days to make sure the bottom of the pit is still submerged in water. After about 8 to 12 weeks, you should see roots starting to develop and grow into the vessel. Not long after that, a stem will emerge and begin to grow from the top of the pit.

8 Once the root system is about 6in/15cm long and strong and healthy, and the stem has started to grow vigorously, your new plant can be transitioned into soil. Take a plastic nursery pot or terra-cotta planter that's 6in/15cm in diameter and fill it with a mix of 70% coco coir, 20% vermiculite, and 10% perlite. Pat this mix down to make sure it's nice and tight. Then make a little hole in the center with just enough room to hold the pit and root system. Carefully place the root system and pit in this hole, making sure that the top half of the pit remains above the surface of the soil. Now that your avocado plant is potted, place it in a spot in your home that receives plenty of direct sun and water it when dry.

ROOT DEVELOPMENT

Once you've taken a cutting, there are a few ways of helping it to develop roots. You can place the cutting directly into water (the most common method), potting mix, perlite, or moss. The choice of medium will be based on the type of plant you are propagating. While some plants will happily put down roots in whichever medium you prefer, others can only be propagated in a particular way. Roots won't appear overnight, though, so be patient and trust that carrying out all the necessary routine maintenance will lead to your plant developing a healthy root system.

IN WATER

Water propagation is known to have the best results over all other methods. And for me, that's very much been the case. To be honest, if I were given a cutting of an extremely rare plant from an extremely rare friend or loved one, and I knew I only had one chance to propagate it or the plant would be as lost to the world as the dinosaurs, I'd put that cutting in water. While no method can guarantee success, propagating in water, whenever possible, will always be my method of choice.

Once you've taken your cutting, whether stem, tip, or leaf, place it in a vessel filled with lukewarm water. Just as when you're watering roots, lukewarm water is easier on the tissue of the plant and helps ease the cutting through its transition into water.

Be mindful of what part of the plant is submerged. For stem-cut plants, you want to make sure one or more nodes are fully under water. This is important, because on vine plants roots develop from the nodes, not the cut end. So if you're styling your cutting in a shallow vessel, you're going to have to top it up with water often to keep the nodes continuously submerged. Although the cutting won't die if only the cut end is under water, it won't assist good root development.

For tip and leaf cuttings, on the other hand, it's important that the cut end of the plant is submerged, as this is where the roots

HOLY WATER

Some new cuttings go into water to begin the root developing process (opposite left). This cutting is starting to develop roots around the node (opposite right). A prayer plant is forming hair-like roots at the base of the node (above). The cuttings in these test tubes have been developing roots for a while and are ready to be transplanted into soil (right).

will develop. To increase the chances of good root growth, you'll need to prevent the cut end from touching the base of the vessel. A good trick is to catch the stem or branch of your cutting in a clothespin, which you can rest on the rim of the vessel. This will suspend the cutting in water without the cut end touching the bottom.

When I talk about propagating in water, I always get the question: "If overwatering potted plants can cause root rot and kill your plant, why is it OK for the roots of your propagation to sit in water for long periods of time?" That is a great question, and it's one with an easy answer. When a potted plant is overwatered, and water is trapped in the soil for too long, the components in the soil start to break down, causing mold and fungi to form and the roots to rot. But when a cutting is developing roots in water, there are no components to create mold and fungus. While bacteria and algae can form over time, refreshing the water and rinsing off the roots will keep the root systems of your cuttings healthy. (See pages 90–91 for routine maintenance.)

IN SOIL

While it is much easier to see the process of developing roots when cuttings are placed in water, going directly into soil is necessary for certain plants. If you were to take a cutting from a large cactus, for example, you wouldn't place it in water to develop roots. You would make the cut, allow the cut end to dry and callus over, then place it directly into potting mix (see page 129 for more on choosing the right mix for cacti.)

However, soil isn't my preferred rooting medium for many other plants because alternative methods tend to have a higher success rate. Also, when you propagate in water, you have the excitement of seeing the cuttings develop roots. In soil, you're constantly playing a guessing game as to whether the cutting has started to root—it's a case of "wait and see."

Different types of plants require different potting mixtures to help them grow. This is of the utmost importance when propagating cuttings. If the mother plant is a large cactus, for example, you want a mixture that is loose, fast-draining, and sandy—the type of habitat that desert plants prefer. But when propagating a peperomia, you need a mixture that retains moisture—a blend of moss, potting mix, and a little perlite. (See pages 128–131 for more details on selecting the right potting mix.)

You will also need the right planter. Some plants don't like moist soil, while others love it. So placing a cutting in a container made of terra-cotta versus glazed ceramic will make a difference. You should also check whether your chosen planter has a drainage hole in the base. (See pages 132–133 for more details on selecting planters.)

Once you have chosen a planter for your cutting, the process is straightforward.

READY, SET, GROW!

I have just taken this cutting and applied rooting hormone to the bottom (opposite above right). The cutting goes into soil and I am gently packing it in to make sure it stands upright (far left). A small stake will keep the cutting upright (left). Watering in the new cutting (below).

YOU WILL NEED

» **Rooting hormone**
» **Planter with drainage hole**
» **Potting mix**
» **Metal or wooden stake and clips/ gardening Velcro (optional)**
» **Watering can**

1 Take the cutting from its mother plant and dab the cut end in rooting hormone.

2 Fill the planter with your preferred soil. Now create a hole in the soil with your finger and push your cutting into the hole, covering at least 2in/5cm of the stem or vine. If it's a vine plant, make sure at least one node is under the surface.

3 To keep the cutting upright, push a stake down into the soil beside it and attach with clips or Velcro.

4 Water the soil with lukewarm water until it begins to trickle out of the drainage hole.

5 Place your plant in a well-lit spot where it will receive bright indirect light and care for it as you would the mother plant.

IN MOSS

Using sphagnum moss to help a cutting develop roots is a great choice. Sphagnum is a natural medium that holds the moisture necessary for root development and helps aerate roots so that they can breathe better. It has another benefit, too. Roots that develop in water tend to form in a ball or become intertwined, whereas a cutting in sphagnum will grow roots that are wide and perfectly formed for a transition into soil. Whether you're using the tip, stem, or leaf-cut technique, the process is as simple as when using water. Here are the steps to propagate in sphagnum moss.

YOU WILL NEED
» **Plastic or glazed ceramic planter**
» **3 cups/700ml sphagnum moss**
» **Metal or wooden stake and clips/ gardening Velcro (optional)**

1 The goal is that the moss is always moist, so pick a glazed ceramic or plastic planter.

2 Place the sphagnum in a bowl and soak it in lukewarm water until it's nice and wet.

3 Fill the bottom half of your chosen planter with damp moss.

4 Take the cutting and wrap the cut end with more damp moss until the nodes or stem are completely surrounded by it. Pack in moss around the cutting to keep it in place in the planter.

MOSS IS THE BOSS

A new *Philodendron* 'Painted Lady' cutting. There are no roots yet, and the stem is bare (opposite above). Here's the same cutting after several weeks growing in sphagnum moss (right). The roots are lush and long after developing in this soft medium.

5 If your cutting is on the large side, use a small stake to keep it upright. Attach it to the cutting with clips or gardening Velcro.

6 Place the cutting in bright indirect light and keep the moss moist by watering it every few days.

As with any medium, root development will happen at its own pace, so be patient. After a few weeks, most plants should have started to put down some roots. If you want to see whether this has occurred, pulling the cutting very gently out of the moss won't hurt it. But remember that the longer roots are allowed to develop, the easier their path will be when transferred into soil.

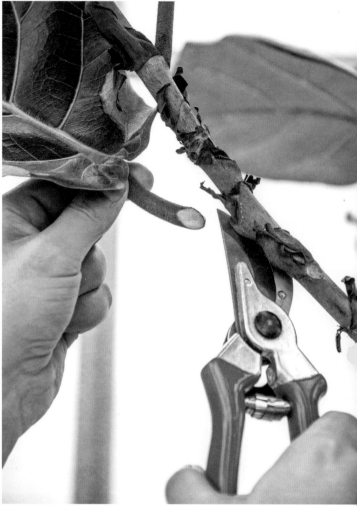

AIR LAYERING

This lesser-used propagation technique involves scoring into a tree-like plant to encourage root development. Air layering is most often used to propagate ficus, sansevierias, citrus, olive trees, dieffenbachias, and crotons (*Codiaeum variegatum*).

It can be less reliably successful than methods in which you remove a cutting from a mother plant. However, what's great about air layering is that there isn't much risk of harming the plant. If you are unsuccessful and the roots fail to develop, your plant will still continue to grow and, in some cases, produce a new branch.

As with other methods for developing roots, this one is a fairly simple process. Here is the step-by-step method for air layering.

YOU WILL NEED
» **Sharp pair of shears/cutting tool**
» **3 cups/700ml sphagnum moss**
» **Large bowl**
» **Plastic wrap/clingfilm**
» **Twine**

1 Select a healthy branch on your plant on which to perform the process. Look for one with bright foliage and new growth.

2 Locate where you want to develop the roots and, with a sharp tool, remove the last leaf on that part of the branch.

3 With the sharp tool, above the leaf scar that you just made, score into the branch slowly until you start to see sap form around the blade. Be careful not to cut too deeply, as this could kill the branch. Wipe the sap away from the wound—it may be toxic to animals and children.

4 Place the sphagnum moss in a bowl and soak it in lukewarm water until saturated.

5 Meanwhile, use twine to tightly tie one end of a piece of plastic wrap/clingfilm to the branch, below the wound.

NEW CUTTING, WHO DIS?
Once I've lopped off a branch, I pick a spot for a second incision and cut into the plant just enough to leave a mark (opposite above right and above). Making preparations to air layer the new incision (right).

6 Wring out handfuls of sphagnum moss so that it is damp but not dripping wet. Wrap the moss around the wound and branch.

7 Pull the plastic wrap/clingfilm over the moss and branch and tie the other end with twine to secure the moss and retain moisture.

8 Check your plant a few times a week to make sure the moss is moist and look for signs of root growth. If the moss is drying out, loosen the plastic wrap, pour a little water inside, and retie it tightly again.

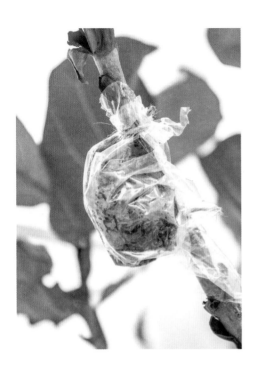

9 Stay patient—this process can take 6 to 10 weeks, depending on the plant. Over time you should start to notice roots making their way through the moss.

10 Once roots have developed, take a sharp blade and cut an inch below the root system, removing the whole branch from the mother tree. Your next move is to transition it into soil (see pages 134–137 for information on how to transition cuttings into soil).

IT'S ALIVE!
Packing sphagnum moss that has been soaked in water and wrung out around the incision on the stem (opposite top right). After six weeks you should start to see roots starting to develop (this page).

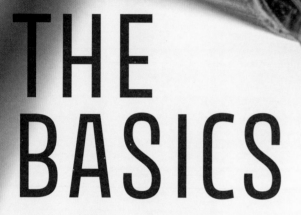

THE
BASICS

Once you've placed your cuttings in the medium that's optimal for root development, some simple routine maintenance will be needed to ensure the plant stays healthy. To succeed at propagation (and indeed at plant parenthood), it's important to have a basic understanding of how to care for your plants. Take note of the advice in this chapter, and your cuttings should soon be well on their way to developing a healthy root system and flourishing new growth.

WATER IS LIFE

This *Philodendron* 'Painted Lady' cutting is being propagated in sphagnum moss in a glazed ceramic planter to help retain moisture. Keeping the moss moist is important for the health of the cutting. Rinsing the roots of an orchid cactus (*Epiphyllum*) cutting to remove bacteria and grime (opposite left). A *Hoya carnosa* 'Albomarginata' cutting has developed roots and is ready for planting (opposite right).

WATER

There are two things that initially matter most when tending to potted plants indoors—the right type of light and the appropriate amount of water. Water is essential to the health of a potted plant, and when propagating it means just as much. It can determine whether cuttings survive and thrive or simply die.

When cuttings are developing roots in water, the water can become a little murky, growing algae and bacteria over time. To avoid this, refresh your vessels with clean water once a week. Not only should you provide your cutting with clean water but clean out the vessel too. A simple rinse with warm water and mild dish soap will do the trick. When propagating in test tubes, I use a small dish brush or bottle brush to remove any grime in the base of the tube.

Refreshing the water presents the perfect opportunity to take cuttings out of their vessels and wash the roots to remove any traces of algae or bacteria. Place the cutting in a sink or bowl and rinse it under lukewarm water, gently moving your fingers across the fragile roots to wash away as much as you can. Do this once every two weeks to maintain a healthy root system.

When propagating in water, it can be easy to forget that the water will evaporate over time. It's important to remember to top up the vessel so that the cut end or node stays submerged. In my home, I check the water level of my cuttings once a day. That may seem excessive, but achieving success happens through work, not by accident.

LIGHT

I've said it before, and I'll say it again—light is everything to every plant. So placing cuttings in the right light will determine whether they thrive... or find their way to the nearest compost bin.

The best type of light for successful propagation is bright indirect light. There are two key words here—BRIGHT and INDIRECT. Bright, meaning the intensity of light, and indirect meaning, well...indirect. It's filtered light that is reflected from the sun. When you place a white sheet or curtain between the sun and a plant, the light that falls on the plant goes from bright and direct to bright and indirect.

Imagine yourself standing in a field on a sunny day. You're fully exposed to the sun. You see the sun, and the sun can see you. That's direct light. Now imagine it's a cloudy day. Thanks to the clouds, the light is evenly diffused and there are no harsh shadows. That's bright indirect light. If a plant can look out the window and see open sky but isn't in direct sunlight, it is in bright indirect light. However, just because a plant is sitting in a window doesn't mean it's getting bright light. There could be a large tree or high building outside that window, reducing the level of light flowing in. Remember, the more open sky that a plant can see, the brighter the light it will receive.

In the northern hemisphere, north-facing windows that look out to open sky provide bright indirect sunlight all day. East-facing windows have direct sun in the morning, then bright indirect sunlight in the afternoon. South-facing windows have a mix of bright indirect and direct sunlight, depending on the time of year and weather conditions, and

These mounted wall cradles hold assorted cuttings and are receiving bright indirect light (left). The darkness of the shadow on the wall behind indicates the intensity of light. When any clear vessel is exposed to bright light it is more likely to develop algae, so make sure to change the water regularly to avoid any buildup of algae or bacteria (above).

west-facing windows have bright indirect sunlight in the morning and direct sun in the afternoon. Naturally, the reverse is true in the southern hemisphere. If you can place your cuttings in bright indirect light, it provides them with the energy to push out healthy root systems at a faster rate.

While different potted plants vary in the intensity of illumination that they need to live healthy lives, a cutting from any plant should never be placed in direct sun. This will heat up the water in the vessel and cause bacteria to build up faster. It will also dry out moss or soil, dehydrating the tissues of your cutting and hindering root growth.

MAINTENANCE

As mentioned, a healthy propagation requires a little regular maintenance. Yes, this adds to your plant care routine, but your new little cuttings are well worth the time and effort.

Tend to the foliage of your cuttings by wiping the leaves down with lukewarm water once a week. This will remove any dust or grime that has settled on the foliage and, more importantly, allow for more light to reach the tissues of the foliage. Remember, light is everything to plant life, so even the smallest bit of extra exposure is beneficial. Routinely wiping down foliage also helps to prevent pest infestations.

While your cuttings are developing roots, don't be surprised if some of the lower leaves start to yellow and fall off. This doesn't mean that the cutting is dying, or that you did something wrong. It might be losing leaves as it needs to divert its energy toward growing roots, so pruning away dying leaves as soon as they start turning yellow is ideal.

Be aware of brown spots developing in the foliage, as this could be a sign that your cutting isn't getting enough light or the root system isn't healthy and needs help. If this is the case, you'll want to cut your propagation where it's still healthy and remove any dying parts. This could mean cutting away the entire root system and starting anew. I know that's not the ideal situation and that's why it's important to perform routine maintenance on your plant babies.

PRIM AND PROPER
Hoya carnosa 'Albomarginata' getting a wipedown (opposite). Check young cuttings regularly. Spraying the leaves with neem oil will deter pests and give them a shiny finish. Brown edges are developing on a *Philodendron xanadu* (above right), while a kangaroo fern is getting a trim (right). Removing brown edges allows the plant to focus on producing growth.

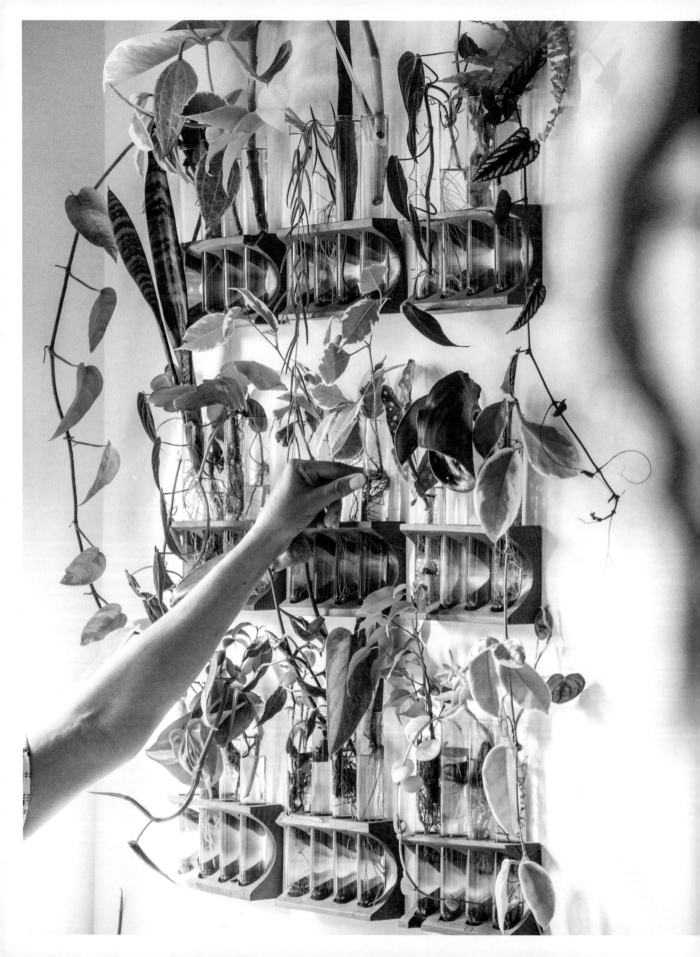

PROPAGATING
in STYLE

MAKE IT BEAUTIFUL

It's one thing to propagate your plants, but it's another to do it with style. It just wouldn't be right for me to share everything I know about propagating plants without also sharing some of my tips and tricks on how to make the whole process look good.

In my last book, *Living Wild*, I showed how color, texture, and shape can bring a space to life, and how important a role they play when it comes to styling plants. I like to bring exactly the same level of detail to the process of propagation. Whether a cutting is resting in a graceful antique vase or potted in a custom-made metal planter, its relationship to other items is relevant. Anyone can take a cutting and stick it in a glass of water, but are you taking into consideration the way in which the texture and shape of that vessel complements the colors and form of the foliage that dances above it? If so, you're on your way to a more rewarding propagating experience and a more beautiful home.

Don't get me wrong: even propagating in a water glass will result in the growth of roots and give you the end result you're hoping for. But cuttings that are styled with intention and flair will provide us with a greater sense of enjoyment and creativity. In this chapter, I share a few of my favorite ways to propagate in style. We'll take a look at what a living wall made from cuttings looks like, learn how to make cutting bouquets, see how single pops of color can create decorative vignettes, find beauty in repurposed objects, and discover how to bring drama and flair with a statement cutting.

STANDING OUT
A large *Philodendron selloum* cutting in an amber glass vase makes a bold statement in the kitchen (opposite). A cutting of *Philodendron bernardopazii* (above right). A bouquet created using propagated houseplants (right).

CREATING LIVING WALLS

When I first had the idea of creating a living wall in my home, my wife and I were living in an apartment and there wasn't much we could do to change the space. We certainly couldn't build in an irrigation system and have plants growing from felt pockets on the wall. So, after considering various ways to create the effect of a living wall without altering the structure of the apartment, I decided to style the wall using vessels I'd designed to hold plant cuttings in water. This created the effect of a lush wall of foliage, but also allowed us to get our security deposit back when we moved out.

Regardless of the type of vessels you plan to use to create a living wall of cuttings, you'll have to be cautious with how you maintain the health of the developing root systems. As explained in the previous chapter, routine maintenance is key, and when you have a wall covered with vessels, replenishing them with fresh water can seem like a constant chore.

To protect the surface of the wall from moisture damage, I used a water-resistant paint, added felt tabs to the back of the wooden cradles, and remained vigilant to prevent any vine plants from attaching their nodes to the wall. While you can find various types of wall-mounted propagation vessels, the beauty in creating a living wall is that it not only helps you grow a large number of plants in your home, but also means you are able to share a piece of your home with others, quite literally.

WOW FACTOR

I designed this propagation station in collaboration with Target back in 2021 (opposite, above, and above right). Mounting propagation vessels on your wall is an easy and inexpensive way to create a living wall in a room and make your space feel unique. There are many vessels out there in the world to choose from, and it is important that you create the right look for you. The propagation station allows you to display 18 small cuttings on your wall to add color, life, and depth to a space and later to give to your loved ones. Single vessels from the same collection can also be combined to make a living wall (right).

SHORT CUTS

We've all heard the old adage, "Good things come in small packages," and when it comes to propagating small cuttings in equally petite vessels, there has never been a more truthful statement. They are a great way to add a touch of life and color to any nook, cranny, or corner of your home. These propagations may be small, but they can have a large impact on your home styling. When a cutting is selected with intention, it can create the perfect vignette and allow for a burst of lush green life in a spot where there may not be enough space for a full-grown plant.

Whether you're snipping a single leaf from a polka dot begonia (*Begonia maculata*) or cutting the very tip of a ZZ plant, you can choose to harmonize or contrast the color and shape of that cutting with the surrounding decor. As always, the vessel your cutting is displayed in plays an important role. Just as you'd always try to pair a mother plant with a stylistically complementary planter, an awareness of how the vessel connects with the cutting is key to great styling.

On the subject of how a vase, pot, or other vessel connects with your cutting, something to be mindful

of when styling these cute little cuttings is that you'll need to top up their water levels frequently. Of course, smaller vessels hold smaller amounts of water, which can evaporate fast, depending on the amount of light the cutting receives or the amount that's taken in by the roots. New cuttings that haven't developed roots yet won't absorb as much water as cuttings with roots. So be aware that while the water level should remain fairly stable around a new cutting, as the roots develop, you'll need to replenish the water levels more often.

SMALL WONDERS

A single stem cutting of a *Tradescantia fluminensis* 'Tricolor' being propagated in one of my single maple cradles (above). This dainty *Syngonium* 'Tricolor Red Spot' cutting sits in a single propagation vessel from my 2021 Target collection (above right). When I'm thinking about how to add life to my space, I start by looking for where the light is but I also consider the surrounding colors and textures (right). Here I've taken a single leaf cutting of a silver satin pothos (*Scindapsus pictus* 'Argyraeus') to add a pop of green to this side table. A ZZ plant stem in an amber glass vessel on a dotted plate creates a colorful moment (opposite).

REPURPOSED

NEW LEASE OF LIFE
A *Philodendron scandens* 'Brasil' vine cascades down the side of an old science beaker in a north-facing window (opposite). A single-stem cutting of a *Tradescantia fluminensis* 'Tricolor' propagated in a repurposed soda bottle (above left). A *Philodendron* 'Florida Green' cutting in a vintage laboratory vessel (above).

Whether you like to call it upcycling, recycling, reusing, or repurposing, having the ability to find treasure in another person's "trash" brings huge benefits for the health of our planet. Don't get me wrong; I like the look and feel of something shiny and new just as much as the next person, but being able to look at a used item and find a cool and creative way to give it a second life is special.

My personal style has always been a little vintage mixed in with a little of the new. I think it's the balance of the two that I find so appealing. While styling my own space, I've always tried to think of ways to repurpose items that weren't getting much use, or things that would normally be tossed out with the trash. Sometimes you just have to look a little deeper to recognize the potential an item might hold. In repurposing, not only do you keep that item out of landfill, but you also make your home more unique and creative. Here are some ways in which you can repurpose items in your home or pieces you might find at thrift stores to help propagate your plants.

VINTAGE GLASSWARE

For me, every glass object I come across has the potential to become a propagation vessel. I mean, why not? All you need is a clean glass vessel filled with water and a cutting taken from your favorite plant. So when I stumble across vintage bottles or clear vases, I immediately consider how they might house my cuttings.

What's great about glassware is that it comes in such a wide variety of different shapes and sizes. From equipment used in the field of science and medicine to bottles created for beverage consumption, they all have a functional beauty of their own. Propagation leans heavily on the side of biology, so placing a cutting in a laboratory beaker or old medicine bottle feels like a perfect fit. I have a soft spot for vintage

beverage containers and the way their labels were either painted on or molded into the glass, giving them an extra pop of color and nostalgia.

But maybe that vintage/used look isn't your thing, and you like to keep it sleek and modern? In that case, I'm sure you have nice glassware hidden away in cabinets that is rarely used. In our home, for example, we have more champagne glasses than any normal household should, so to mix a little new in with the old, I'll take out a champagne flute and use it as a propagation vessel. Now you've classed it up and truly have something to celebrate! With all the different types of glassware out there, you really could create your own unique propagation station that will be to die for. Or, better said, to live for!

OLD MEETS NEW

In the Good Neighbor Guesthouse in Baltimore, Maryland, I styled a few plant cuttings in propagation vessels. Creating a new look with used or repurposed objects suited the way the guesthouse was renovated to make the old new again. I placed a polka dot begonia in an old wine bottle and a Rex begonia in a small vintage pharmacy bottle (opposite left and right). A *Ficus benjamina* 'Variegata' cutting is presented in a used tequila bottle (above). Another vintage bottle pairs perfectly with the tile it sits on and has a pattern that resembles that of the umbrella tree it holds (above right). And a *Dracaena reflexa* 'Song of India' branch is held upright in a tall glass vessel (right).

STATEMENT PIECES

We never get a second chance at making a first impression. The first chance is all we get, so it's important to make that moment count. Make it memorable. Make a statement. When it comes to styling your interior space, it's a must.

If you've read any of my previous books, you'll be familiar with my love for a statement plant. I don't categorize a plant as such due to its size, but because in some way it commands the eye and demands admiration. This could be down to a plant's vibrant color, intricate patterns, boldly shaped foliage, or interesting texture, all or any of which will make it stand out from the crowd. Usually, statement plants are potted in soil. But here I want to talk about statement cuttings. Yes, that's right—a stand-out cutting that will create a talking point in any interior.

A statement cutting works in exactly the same way as a statement houseplant. It demands our attention and anchors the room (or part of the room) that it occupies. But a statement cutting is visually intriguing not only because of the plant it comes from, but also due to the manner in which it's styled. As you've seen in this chapter, choosing the right vessel is key when styling propagations.

While some statement plants are large in stature, cuttings do not have size on their side, so making a statement relies entirely on their appearance. When I want to make a statement with a cutting, I start by looking for interesting parts of the plant that stand out. That might be down to a curve in the stem or the wild weirdness of aerial roots protruding from a vine—when I spot such things, the statement begins to formulate in my mind. Then I finish it off by choosing a container that helps accentuate the wild beauty of the cutting, giving it space to show off its good looks and lift it up for all to appreciate.

BOUQUETS

There are few things that can brighten up a space visually and aromatically like a bouquet of fresh-cut florals. Such a bouquet is like the cherry on the top of a sundae, or the sprinkles on a cupcake—the last added touch of goodness that brings a living space together.

Recently, floral design has become extremely popular, with many designers using their creativity to construct what I can only describe as floral sculptures: living works of art that bloom from their vases. Personally, the reason I rarely bring cut flowers home is because they are here today and gone tomorrow.

The lifespan of a cut flower is short, and the moment of enjoyment flickers out like embers of burning wood floating into the night sky. I prefer growing plants that make my spaces feel warm and inviting, because I know that with proper care, I can keep them alive year after year. That being said, I started to think about creative ways to take cuttings from plants and style them in vases before giving them a new life. A way to allow them to live for a good amount of time in water while developing roots and then being potted in a new planter. I'm talking about propagation.

A tip cutting of *Ficus elastica* 'Tineke' in a gorgeous handmade vessel (this page). The variegation in the ficus plays really well with the white of the vase and complements its organic feel. In a gold vase, stems of *Monstera deliciosa* 'Thai Constellation', ZZ plant, *Philodendron scandens* 'Brasil', and *Monstera adansonii* all sit happily together (opposite).

DIY BOUQUETS

Why not use your creativity and plant knowledge to take cuttings from your houseplants and arrange them in a beautiful bouquet to sit atop your dining table, kitchen table, entryway, or anywhere that needs a pop of color, life, or creativity? The process of creating and arranging bouquets for your home, whether with cut florals or cut houseplants, can be very therapeutic and calming and provide you with a deeper appreciation for being a plant parent.

In order to do so, there are a few things you'll need to know. When you're taking a cutting from your plant, you're not only considering how your bouquet will be arranged when gathered together in a vase but how its mother plant will look right after the cut is made and then grow down the road. This forces you to slow down and really hone in and be more intentional with where you choose to make the cuts and how much of a cut should be taken (for more on this, see pages 16–57).

Then you'll need to pair those cuttings with a vessel that will speak perfectly to the theme or vibe you're looking to convey. And then finally it's about finding the right light for the bouquet to make its statement but also thrive. All of this feels quite Zen to me. I've always had respect for florists, but in creating propagation bouquets, I've gained a whole new level of appreciation for the wonderful works of art they create. So, with that said, here are a few tips on how to go about creating your own cuttings for bouquets.

FLY DIY

Making a bouquet out of cuttings should be done with purpose and with a well thought-out theme in mind (opposite). This moody bouquet sets the tone for an elegant dinner party. Ensuring every part of the arrangement shines takes frequent reworking and adjusting, but with a propagating bouquet, you will have a beautiful centerpiece for months (above).

1 What's the vibe? The first thing I do when creating a bouquet from cuttings is make a decision on the color palette. Here I'm going for a moodier vibe, so I'm using plants on the darker side.

2 Find your light Your number one question when styling a bouquet of cuttings should always be, "Where should I place this bouquet to give the plants the best opportunity to thrive and develop roots?" Here, I decided to design a bouquet for the center of my dining table. This space enjoys medium light for most of the day, so I'm using plants that can tolerate or thrive in those conditions.

3 Select your vessel Choosing the right vessel when designing your bouquet is key to completing the look you're going for. Since the mood here is dark and striking, I've selected a fluted smoked glass vase. It will sit in the center of the dining table, so choosing the right size vessel will determine how guests around the table are able to interact.

4 Choose your cuttings Sticking with my theme and light requirements, I've taken cuttings from my Raven ZZ (*Zamioculcas zamiifolia* 'Raven'), polka dot begonia (*Begonia maculata*), *Geogenanthus ciliatus,* and burgundy rubber plant (*Ficus elastica* 'Abidjan'). While the ZZ, geogenanthus, and rubber plant are all similar in color and sheen, their foliage is of different sizes and shapes, which is helpful when creating a full bouquet. I decided to use the rubber plant as the main feature, sitting it higher in the vase, while the Raven ZZ stems fill in the middle and the geogenanthus clusters at the bottom. The polka dot begonia breaks up the solid tones and textures; while its foliage is dark like the rest, its spotted pattern makes it pop and stand out.

5 Preparing your vessel Add the clay pebbles to your vessel, then fill it above halfway with lukewarm water. The clay pebbles will help to hold the cuttings in place and submerged in water.

6 Create your arrangement Start by placing your larger cuttings in the vase first, then gradually work in the rest around them. If your cuttings won't stay in the position you want, add another handful of clay pebbles. The more stems you add, the more likely they are to stay in place. It may take some time to get the look you desire, but eventually you'll have the perfect propagation bouquet.

Care for your bouquet just as you would any propagation placed in water (see pages 78–79).

PLANTED

STEPS TO SUCCESS

How do you measure success? Is it defined by the pursuit of a chosen goal? Or must that goal be achieved? To my mind, even an attempt can be worth celebrating, but when it comes to propagation, you have to look at the results.

For some, successful propagation occurs the moment a cutting starts to produce roots. Personally, I think a propagation is successful when you transition that cutting into soil and see it grow and mature to become a mother plant with the ability to be propagated itself. Full circle.

For this to happen, a cutting must transition into soil once it has developed roots. Think about it. When you purchase a houseplant from a store, it doesn't come with the roots exposed in an empty pot. The roots are always surrounded by soil or another growing medium. And for your new cutting to take the next step in its growth cycle, it will need to be planted into soil, too.

Whenever I'm discussing propagation in a public setting or sharing the process online, I'm often asked the question: "Is it necessary to transition a cutting into soil? Can it just continue to grow in water or moss and stay relatively healthy?". Well, the operative word there is "relatively." Yes, you may be able to keep a cutting in water or moss for a long period of time, but it won't thrive and grow into a mature plant unless its roots are surrounded by soil and it receives the nutrients it needs to grow.

However, there can be many reasons why a cutting might not "take" once it is transitioned into soil. This step in the propagation process is where many of us encounter problems, but often this is purely down to a lack of knowledge regarding how to care for that

READY TO ROOT

The roots of a pothos 'Shangri La' cutting look ready for planting (opposite). The stem of this succulent has been stripped of its lower leaves, forcing it to root at the base (above). When rooting a succulent in water, the key is to use a vessel that is not much bigger than the cutting.

particular plant. As long as you take the time to understand what it needs, you will be fine.

Like many things in life, there is a right way, a wrong way, and, of course, there is your way. We all hope our way aligns with the right way more often than not. When the time comes to move your newly propagated plant into soil, the following pages will show you how best to proceed.

SOIL MATTERS

The rule of (green) thumb is to transition a plant into a pot that is 2in/5cm larger in diameter than its previous pot. But this is propagation, so you'll have to gauge the right size of pot based on the size of the plant's root system. And before you can decide how much soil is needed to fill that pot, you need to know the kind of soil mixture that's right for your plant. Remember, the moisture level of the soil will tell you when to water your plant. So providing your plant with the right potting mix is everything. To help you give your plants the soil they need, here are my tips for creating the right potting mix.

FOR PHILODENDRON, POTHOS, MONSTERAS, DRACAENAS, MOST PALMS, AND FICUS

When adding soil to these plants, I always have a bag of organic potting mix ready to go. Philodendron and ficus like their soil to be moist for a day or two after watering, then to dry out in the top half of their pots, so for those plants I create a custom blend that's 80% potting mix and 20% perlite, in order to ensure good drainage. However, I will also take the container into account. If planting a ficus in a non-porous ceramic glazed pot, which will retain more moisture in the soil, I would add another 10% perlite (or sand) to compensate.

FOR FERNS, ANTHURIUMS, PEPEROMIAS, BEGONIAS, GOEPPERTIAS, AND CALATHEAS

These plants like their soil to stay evenly moist, so I make up a blend of 70% potting mix, 20% sphagnum moss, and 10% vermiculite or bark. Personally, I wouldn't place any of these plants in a porous container, as the material will draw moisture from the soil and your plant's roots. If you decide to do so, adjust your blend to contain another 10% sphagnum moss and remember that you'll need to water your plant more frequently.

FOR CACTI, SUCCULENTS, SNAKE PLANTS, ZZ PLANTS, AND PONYTAIL PALMS

These plants want their soil to be dry for long periods between watering and require a fast-draining mix. I make sure to have a bag of organic potting mix, a bag of perlite, and a bag of sand readily available and mix the three together in equal quantities to create the right blend. In most cases, slightly increasing the quantity of perlite is helpful. Cacti and succulents tend to grow best in porous containers, but if you want to place them in a plastic or glazed container, I'd change the proportions of the soil to 35% perlite, 35% sand, and 30% potting mix.

THE RIGHT MIX

This peperomia cutting is ready to be transplanted in a new medium containing soil, sphagnum moss, and vermiculite—a water-retaining mineral (opposite). Having potting mix on hand is a must (above). It's a great foundation for many mixes because you can add other mediums or minerals to make the perfect mix for your houseplants. Here I have made a blend of perlite, peat-free moss, and a general container mix (above and right). Perlite is great for adding aeration and drainage. Most potting mixes already have some perlite in them, but you can add more based on your plants' specific needs.

TYPES OF SOIL MIXES

There is a world of potting mediums out there aside from just "soil." Pumice, silt, loam, clay, humus, sand, wool, bark, charcoal, coco coir, sphagnum, vermicompost, lava rock, gravel—the list goes on. Different plants thrive in different mediums, so creating your own mixture for an individual plant's needs is the sign of a good green caregiver. Start simple: learn what kind of plant you have, research its origins, and gather your materials from there.

1 Soil Standard soil mixes usually include some sort of compost, perlite, a peat substitute, and maybe sand (below).

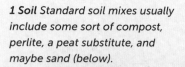

2 Perlite This is an organic material made of volcanic glass. It's used to improve drainage and airflow to root systems (above).

3 Vermiculite Add this to your potting mixture to encourage water retention. It holds onto excess water in the soil so you don't need to water as often (below).

4 Coco coir Made from coconut fiber, coco coir retains moisture and promotes healthy roots. It's an eco-friendly alternative to peat moss (left).

PICKING
THE PLANTER

Please understand this: all planters are not created equal. The material that the planter is made from will dictate how much moisture and air are present in the soil that surrounds your plant and consequently how much will be able to reach the roots. If you place your precious new cutting in the right planter, you've set yourself up for success.

POROUS CONTAINERS

Containers made from porous materials like clay, terra-cotta, concrete, and most woods are breathable and absorbent, meaning they allow air to move through them better than other materials and draw moisture away from the soil, allowing it to dry faster. Plants such as cacti, succulents, ficus, pothos, and philodendron, just to name a few, can benefit from being planted in a porous container.

SOLID CONTAINERS

Plastic, glazed ceramic, and even metal planters are the opposite of their porous counterparts. Air and water cannot pass through them so they help to retain moisture in the soil. Plants like begonias, alocasias, ferns, calatheas and goeppertias, anthuriums, and so on—anything that likes its soil to stay evenly moist—would be happiest in containers made from these materials.

NURSERY POTS

Another alternative is planting your cuttings directly into nursery pots. I mean, why not? Every new plant you bring home more than likely comes in one of these plastic containers. While many people instantly repot their plants and toss the plastic nursery pots in the trash, I always keep a stack of them around. They are perfect for propagated cuttings once they have developed roots and it is time to pot them on.

THE PERFECT PAIRING

Planters come in all shapes and sizes (opposite, above and right). When choosing a plant to match your container, height is important to keep in mind. This *Begonia maculata* has very colorful foliage and stands tall (above right). Pairing it in a pot that is taller than it is wide will ensure it stays upright for longer.

THE TRANSITION

When the time comes to plant your rooted cutting into soil, you're going to use exactly the same process as you would when repotting an established plant. Now that you know how to cook up the right soil mixture for your plant and have selected a planter made from the right material to help support your plant's root system, it's pretty straightforward. You've repotted a plant before, right? No? Well, here's how to go about planting your propagation:

YOU WILL NEED
» **Ruler**
» **Planter (see below)**
» **The correct potting mix for your plant (see pages 128–129)**
» **Small gardening spade**
» **Gloves**
» **Small wooden stake and string or Velcro plant tie (optional)**
» **Watering can filled with water**

1 Measure with a ruler to help you find a pot that's the right size for your new plant. With the top of your cutting in one hand and the root system in the other, loosely ball the roots up and measure the width. You need a planter that is 2in/5cm in diameter larger than the root ball. Don't be tempted to graduate straight to a larger pot—cuttings prefer to be a little snug.

2 Scoop some of your fresh potting mix into the pot, filling up the bottom third and patting it down. Place the cutting in the pot, gently coaxing and spreading its new roots out over the surface of the soil.

3 Gently scoop more soil on top of
the roots until they are completely
covered. Leave the uppermost
10 percent of the pot free of soil,
to prevent it from overflowing when
you water the plant.

HOYA JOY

**This *Hoya carnosa* 'Algomarginata' has a very
established root system and is ready to be
planted in soil (opposite and this page). Like
succulents, hoyas need a free-draining mixture
and a porous planter, like this terra-cotta pot,
so they can dry out between waterings.**

4 Gently pat the top layer of soil down to make sure that the cutting is secure in its new home. If the cutting seems too heavy to stand up straight on its own, use a small plant stake and gently push it into the soil. Then take a small length of string or a Velcro plant tie and attach the cutting to the stake to give it additional support. Once the roots of the cutting have grown longer and stronger and the cutting is supporting its own weight, the stake can be removed.

5 Water the cutting as needed (see below) and make sure it receives the appropriate levels of light while it acclimatizes to its new surroundings. During this period, don't be surprised if your plant loses a few leaves. This is your plant's way of letting you know that it's going to shed anything that it can't support in its new environment. Once it settles down, you should see less leaf loss, and if all is done correctly, you'll begin to see new growth in no time.

AFTERCARE

It's important to understand that just because this plant is the same as the mother plant it came from, this does not mean it needs watering on the same schedule. This is one of the biggest mistakes plant parents make when transitioning propagations into soil. The new cutting you just planted is much smaller, with a smaller root system surrounded by less soil, and the pot it's in will dry up much faster. For example, if you have a mature *Philodendron scandens* 'Brasil' in an 8in/20cm pot that you water once a week, and now you have a cutting from that plant in a 4in/10cm pot, you'll more than likely need to water it twice a week. Get this right, and you'll be on the path to a successful propagation and a brand-new member of your plant family.

AU PAIR PLANT CARE
When you propagate a new plant, it's like having a toddler you need to keep an eye on (above and opposite). That means extra attention around the clock, with frequent watering and pest checks, until it establishes roots and enters the teenager phase.

DIY KOKEDAMA MOSS BALL

There are so many beautiful varieties of plant out there to propagate, and so many incredible planters to grow them in once they have developed roots. But there is no potting style more unique than a *kokedama*—*koke* meaning "moss" in Japanese and *dama*, which means "ball". This traditional method of potting a plant in moss has been around for centuries, but has experienced a surge of popularity in recent years. While it is mainly used for smaller plants, so that the *kokedama* can be suspended in your home like a hanging planter, the same technique can be applied to bigger houseplants as well. *Kokedama*, both large and small, look great when placed on the floor or a table.

Certain plants respond and thrive better when surrounded by particular materials, and not every plant wants to be cultivated in the *kokedama* style. Some of my favorite cuttings to use are philodendrons, pothos, ferns, peperomias, and anthuriums. These all tolerate or thrive in soil that leans on the moist side and tend to grow a little slower than others.

What's different about a plant styled in a *kokedama* rather than in a typical clay planter is that the plant is wrapped in moss, a natural material that has a lush and organic feel, whether it's sitting on a tabletop or hanging from the ceiling. And as it's not in a pot, you have more options when it comes to styling it in the home. When the time comes to transition cuttings of these plants into soil, this is a fun and unexpected way to do so.

KOKEDAMA DRAMA
The acid-green foliage of *Philodendron* 'Lemon Lime' makes for a dramatic contrast with the darker hue of the moss ball (opposite). I have placed it on a shelf in a corner that receives medium to low indirect light, which this plant appreciates (above).

YOU WILL NEED
- » Plant cutting
- » Bonsai potting mix
- » Water
- » Coco coir potting mix
- » Sphagnum moss (or preserved moss)
- » Twine
- » Sharp pair of shears/ cutting tool
- » Shallow base tray or plate made of a non-porous material such as glazed ceramic

1 You'll need a cutting that's already developed a good root system. Here I'm using a *Philodendron* 'Lemon Lime' that has been propagated in water.

2 On a flat surface, combine 80% bonsai potting mix with 20% coir potting mix. The moss will help to retain moisture around the roots of the cutting. Slowly pour a little water over the mixture, pressing it together to form a ball.

3 Don't feel defeated if the soil doesn't come together instantly. Keep on adding water little by little until you have the right consistency, and the soil starts to clump into a clay-like mixture. Once it holds together, form it into a ball that's 2in/5cm larger in diameter than the root ball of your cutting. The root ball of my cutting is approximately 2in/5cm in diameter, so here I am forming a ball that's 4in/10cm in diameter.

4 Once the ball is holding together well, test its stability by tossing it gently into the air and catching it. If it stays in one piece, you're all set, but if it's crumbling or collapsing, add more water and press it into shape again.

5 Gently break the soil ball into two halves.

6 Take the cutting and position the roots between the two halves of the ball, then tightly bring them together around the roots. Pack the soil in around the base of the stem, making sure the ball is tightly packed and the roots are completely encased in soil. If the ball feels a little dry or crumbly, slowly add a few more drops of water and form it again. Place it to one side.

7 Put the sphagnum moss in a bowl and pour over some water. Let it soak for a few moments, then wring it out. You want it to be damp, not dripping wet. Spread out the moss in a ½in/1cm-thick layer on the work surface and place the ball of soil right in the center.

8 Gently wrap the moss around the ball to make sure you have enough. If it doesn't provide adequate coverage, repeat the previous step until you have the right amount. Now wrap the moss around the ball, covering all the soil.

9 Cut a 2ft/60cm length of twine. Starting at the top, close to the stem of the cutting, start to wrap the twine around the moss-covered soil ball, working your way from the top of the ball to the bottom and back up again. The objective is to hold the moss in place. Secure the ball by knotting the twine and trimming any excess.

10 And so you have it—your very own *kokedama*! Traditionally it would be suspended with twine, but I prefer to keep mine where they are easy to style and care for. Place your *kokedama* on a non-porous tray or plate so that the moisture stays on top of the tray and isn't absorbed. Depending on the amount of light your plant needs to thrive, you might want to position it on top of a kitchen counter, a coffee table, or, as I've done with my cutting, on a bookshelf.

AFTER CARE

When it comes to caring for your *kokedama*, you're going to want to keep it on the moist side. Check if it needs to be watered by picking it up—if it feels light, it needs water. Let the ball sit in a bowl or sink filled with lukewarm water for 10 to 15 minutes. After that, place it back on its tray. Any runoff water will be held in the tray and gradually absorbed.

Take note of any signs that your plant might need a little extra TLC. If its leaves start turning yellow, this means you're not letting it dry out enough between waterings. And if the foliage develops dry brown spots on the tips, your plant is not receiving enough moisture. Life is about finding balance, and you'll definitely need to find the balance here.

Since *kokedama* need to be kept moist, it's best to place it in a spot that enjoys indirect light. Just be mindful not to place it in direct sun. This can burn the foliage and kill the plant.

Once you start to notice roots creeping out through the moss or the foliage begins to look a little unhealthy, you'll know that your plant's roots have outgrown the moss ball. Once this happens, carefully remove the twine and moss and create a larger *kokedama* to accommodate the root system as it grows.

ALL ABOUT BALANCE

These variegated plants work nicely together with all the different sizes and textures of their leaves (opposite). In the center sits a jade plant (*Crassula ovata*) in a *kokedama*. The decorative saucer underneath will catch any excess water.

HILTON CARTER WILD GREE

HILTON CARTER WILD INT

WILD AT HOM

THE
GIFT

HANDLE WITH CARE

I might be going out on a limb here, but I believe that there is no better gift for another plant lover than a cutting from one of your own plants. Creating a special bond with plants through propagation has made me excited to gift cuttings to others in my life. I hope that they will also experience the immense joy and passion I feel when bringing plants into my home and will want to pass the gift of propagation on to their own friends and family.

In the previous chapters, I have shared my knowledge, thoughts, and experience about propagating houseplants. While working with plants, I've learned many lessons, but my initial start in propagating was gifted to me. To this day, it's a gift that I've utilized frequently. Because when you gift someone a propagation, not only are you giving them a new plant, but you're also gifting them the knowledge and the means to propagate that plant themselves. Propagation is truly the gift that keeps on giving.

A cutting from a *Philodendron brandtianum* (Brandy, for short) wrapped in a moist paper towel, getting ready to be transported to its new home (opposite, left and above).

When planning to gift a cutting, the key thing to remember is that the cut end of the plant must be kept moist. So once you've made the cut from a plant, or removed a cutting that has already begun to develop roots from a vessel, take a paper towel, wet it with lukewarm water, then gently wrap it around the cut end of the plant or around the developed roots. If you've made a fresh cut, you can secure the paper towel to the plant with a rubber band but if your cutting has roots, I'd suggest going without the rubber band—just let the paper towel caress the roots gently, to avoid damaging the developing root system.

Now place the wrapped stem or branch in a ziplock bag and zip it closed, making sure the plant's foliage is outside the bag. Presenting a cutting like this gives the recipient time to get it home and transfer it to a new vessel. The cutting will survive in the bag for a day or two as long as the paper towel is kept moist.

DIY) PROPAGATION PLACE SETTING

There's nothing that my family and I love more than entertaining at home. So much so that we renovated to accommodate this passion, making our kitchen larger and more conducive to gatherings. For me, life is about creating moments with the ones you love and making them feel special. So from time to time, we pick a theme, decorate the house, and bring friends and family together. And since it's the table that we spend many hours laughing, dining, and sharing stories across, I like to make sure that my table settings create a "wow" moment for our guests.

Once you've decided on a theme for your event—maybe based on color, season, or occasion—you'll want to pick dinnerware, flatware, glassware, and so on to suit it. This is also the time to choose a cutting that will work beautifully with everything else. It could bring a pop of color, or act as a dramatic and unexpected addition to the table. Or maybe it could be a good opportunity to prune back that plant in your home that has gotten a little unruly, or that your visitors have been eyeballing for months.

There are a few things to be mindful of here. Firstly, make sure you're not choosing cuttings that are too large for the table setting. Secondly, don't pick out plants that will be difficult for your guests to care for once they pot them. And lastly, make sure the cuttings are healthy and free of pests. It's a very kind gesture to gift a cutting to a loved one. It's an extremely unkind gesture to gift them an infestation.

Here the theme of my party is a "fall gathering." To bring that to life, I've opted for mustard-colored placemats, textured ceramic plates in an earthy hue, matte black flatware, and clear glassware. Everything here sets the tone for the vibe I'm looking to create.

FEAST YOUR EYES
Cuttings from a Raven ZZ plant styled in cloth napkins bring a tropical feel to the table setting (opposite and above). Your dinner guests will not only leave with a gift, but a memory of the good times you shared.

I'm going to fold the napkins to hold cuttings that function as the main feature, so I've chosen a greige design with a tropical jungle print. To play off the black matte flatware, I've decided to tuck a cutting from *Zamioculcas zamiifolia* 'Raven', the dark-hued Raven ZZ plant, into each napkin as a gift to our dinner guests. This plant is also a practical choice, because it's robust enough to withstand being moved about during the party and traveling home with its new parent at the end of the night. And, as I mentioned on page 51, the ZZ is low maintenance and easy to propagate.

If you'd like to recreate the effect at home, here are a few tips on how to pull it together.

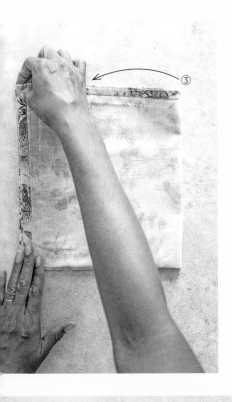

Folding the napkin

1 Open out your napkin and lay it on a flat surface. Make sure to have the right side face up.

2 Now pick up the bottom corners of the napkin and fold it in half to create a rectangle with the patterned or right sides facing. Make sure the edges and corners line up neatly (do this each time you fold).

3 Working from right to left, fold the right edge of the napkin over to the left to make a square.

4 Take the top-left corner of the napkin and peel it back to the bottom right, so the patterned or right side is revealed.

5 Working from left to right, flip the square over so the fold is facing downward.

6 Neatly fold over the right third of the napkin, then fold the left third over that. Tuck the lower right corner into the fold behind it.

7 Flip it over and you have a folded napkin with a pocket, all ready to receive a plant cutting.

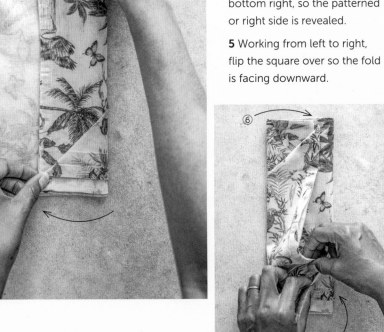

Making the cut

8 Bear in mind that you won't want to leave the cuttings lying out on the table all day, so it's best to take the cuttings an hour or so before the party starts. As the floral water tubes are small in length and diameter, you'll need to take cuttings with slender stems. Make the cut that works best for propagating the plant you're using.

9 Take the caps off the tubes, fill each tube with lukewarm water, and replace the caps.

10 Carefully push your stems or branches through the opening in the cap of the tube. If the stem is slightly larger than the cap's opening, use your shears to widen the opening a little. Take care not to make it any larger than necessary, as then the water will leak out when the tube is placed in the folded napkin.

11 Once each cutting is in its tube, slide every one into a folded napkin and position as desired on the table.

And there is your "wow" moment! Your guests will be blown away by the design and touched by your generosity. Let them know how you came up with the theme of the party and why you chose this particular plant to gift to them. Make sure to share care tips for when they get the cutting home and explain how to transition it into soil once it develops roots. Trust me, they'll love you for it. But don't blame me when you get a reputation as the friend that gives out cuttings at their dinner parties and become the star of the group. Because that's going to happen. See it as my gift to you. You're welcome!

ATTENTION TO DETAIL
I like to match the plant to the occasion. *Cissus discolor* creates a jungle feel (right). Watermelon peperomia tied up with candy-cane twine is perfect for a holiday dinner (below). Rex begonia adds a pop of color to an outdoor table (below right).

LAST NOTES

We came, we saw, we propagated. Well, at least I hope so. In this book, I've shared my knowledge about successfully propagating houseplants and how to 'grow' a plant collection, in all senses of the word. I've walked you through the process of propagating from stem, tip, and leaf cuttings, using the method of division and separation, growing from a seed, and more. We've covered how to care for cuttings while their roots develop and, ultimately, how to transition them into soil for a successful result. However, as with everything in life, there are no guarantees. So, while we hope to propagate one of our favorite plants and see it develop roots and thrive, sometimes it just isn't meant to be. If it doesn't work for you the first time, or even the second, don't be deterred. Through the process of trying, you're setting yourself up for success in the future. Propagating can be difficult and time-consuming, but it is also one of my favorite parts of being a plant parent.

Now that you have the knowledge, it's time to put it to use. As they say, the more you know, the more you grow. While the intention of this book is to equip you with the knowledge to grow your plant family through propagation, my ultimate desire is that you create strong bonds with the plants you share your home with and feel inspired to learn more about how to tend to their needs. I believe the process of propagation teaches all of us how to be a little more patient and to understand the importance of nurturing what nurtures us. It's a wonderful way to open our minds and hearts to all living things and, hopefully, propagate kindness and love.

INDEX

Page numbers in *italic* refer to the illustrations

THANKS

I am so grateful to be part of a community that understands the power that plants can bring to the home and to life in general. Since I started along my journey in greenery, I've been waiting for the opportunity to share my thoughts and ideas on how to propagate houseplants, and I am thankful that that opportunity has finally arrived.

I want to start by thanking my incredible wife, Fiona, because there is no me without her. Fiona, every part of me is made stronger because of you. Watching you care and nurture our little propagation (our daughter) melts me daily. I'm more motivated, passionate, and loving because of you. Thank you.

Holland, you're my heart. I do everything with you in mind. I look forward to the day I get to share the knowledge in this book with you and watch as you become as wild about plants as I am. I love you. To all my family and friends that have been so supportive through everything, from the bottom, top and center of my heart, thank you.

I couldn't have taken many of these images without the helping hands of Jasmen Davis, Ryan Rhodes, and my beautiful mother. Thank you. You were the perfect models of what hand modeling should be. Thanks to Franziska Scherzer and Valentina Massa for letting me photograph your avocado plants. Ryan, thank you for helping with the additional photography and your friendship and support throughout this process. Let's keep going. Thank you Coco Chiosi for helping me stay on task and on

schedule. We're now on this journey together. Carsen Delmont and Mollie Lee, thank you for your help. And thank you to Patty Wilson, who first introduced me to propagating plants.

To the team at CICO Books, thank you again and again for the hard work you put into making our books a success. The relationship we've developed over the years has made every part of the process delightful.

Lastly, I thank every one of you that shares my passion for indoor greenery, creating indoor oases, and living wild. It's your continued support and appreciation that fuels my desire to share what I love.

This book is dedicated to Holland and Sienna.